Fresh Ideas in Letterhead and Business Card Design 3

Fresh Ideas
in Letterhead and
Business Card
Design 3

L Y N N   H A L L E R

NORTH LIGHT BOOKS
CINCINNATI, OHIO

Fresh Ideas in Letterhead and Business Card Design 3. Copyright © 1997
by North Light Books. Printed and bound in Singapore. All rights reserved. No
part of this book may be reproduced in any form or by any electronic or
mechanical means including information storage and retrieval systems without
permission in writing from the publisher, except by a reviewer, who may quote
brief passages in a review. Published by North Light Books, an imprint of
F&W Publications, Inc., 1507 Dana Avenue, Cincinnati, Ohio 45207. (800)
289-0963. First edition.

This hardcover edition of *Fresh Ideas in Letterhead and Business Card Design 3*
features a "self-jacket" that eliminates the need for a separate dust jacket. It provides sturdy protection for your book while it saves paper, trees and energy.

Other fine North Light Books are available from your local bookstore, art sup-
ply store or direct from the publisher.

01   00   99   98   97   5   4   3   2   1

Library of Congress Cataloging-in-Publication Data

Haller, Lynn
     Fresh ideas in letterhead and business card design 3 / Lynn
Haller. — [3rd ed.]
        p.   cm.
     Includes index.
     ISBN 0-89134-784-4 (pob : alk. paper)
     1. Letterheads—Design. 2. Business cards—Design. 3. I. Title.
NC1002.L47H35   1996
741.6—dc20   96-44784
                                                       CIP

Edited by Lynn Haller
Designed by Sandy Conopeotis Kent

The permissions on page 139 constitute an extension of this copyright page.

North Light Books are available for sales promotions, premiums and fund-
raising use. Special editions or book excerpts can also be created to specification.
For details, contact the Special Sales Manager, F&W Publications, 1507 Dana
Avenue, Cincinnati, Ohio 45207.

Table of Contents

From the Editor

This is the third edition of *Fresh Ideas in Letterhead and Business Card Design* that I have worked on in some capacity, and it's probably safe to say that—including the entries featured in these three books, as well as the thousands of entries not accepted for publication—I've seen more letterhead in the past five years than most people will see in a lifetime of correspondence.

But despite this, I continue to be amazed by the possibilities of this medium—its very limitations seem to inspire designers to do some of their most innovative work. Each edition I've worked on has included work that demonstrates new possibilities for this old medium. For instance, I would never have thought of scanning individual hands for the back of each employee's business card—but Rick Eiber Design did (p. 121). I would not have thought of die-cutting a business card in the shape of a leaf—but Studio MD did (p. 57). And I'm sure that when you open this book, you'll discover your own favorites—work whose inventiveness might inspire you to create work fresh enough to appear in the next edition of this book.

As tried and true a medium as letterhead is, each edition of this book continues to be full of surprises, for the editor and for the reader too, I hope.

The Basics of Letterhead Design

Designing letterhead may be among a designer's favorite projects: Where else can a design idea be conveyed so economically, allowing the brilliance of the concept to be uncluttered by coupons, price lists, graphs, or bad photographs supplied by the client? But for that same reason, letterhead is also among the most challenging pieces to design: When working within the strict parameters and—often—the tight budgets that also come with a typical letterhead project, the lack of a good concept will be hard to hide. It's one of the truest tests of your skills as a designer.

This introductory course in letterhead design may not give you the definitive answer on how to come up with a perfect concept, but it will point out the questions you should ask yourself to get there, and what to do with that concept once you've got it.

Getting to Know Your Client

Your first step in designing a letterhead project, as in any other design project, will be to get as much information as possible from your client. It's important to emphasize this when discussing letterhead design, because its very simplicity can lead you to assume that all you need to know is the company name and address. Not true—because of letterhead's importance in conveying an impression (often the first one) of your client, you must take nothing for granted.

Here are some of the questions you'll need to consider before you start designing a letterhead system; your client should be able to answer many of these questions for you, while others might require further thought or research on your part:

- What pieces does your client need designed? Beyond the obvious, list other components related to letterhead that they may not have thought of, such as presentation folders, stickers, invoices, fax cover sheets, etc.; make sure they're aware that the best letterhead design can be undercut when used in conjunction with ill-designed (or undesigned) collateral.
- Did they have a previous letterhead? If so, why do they want a new letterhead? Is there anything they still like about it (the ink colors, the paper) that you should consider retaining?
- What, if any, other corporate identity elements already exist, and does your client intend to keep any of them? If no other components exist, you'll need to consider whether the elements from your letterhead design might eventually be used on other pieces—for instance, if your client is a delivery service, they may eventually want to use design elements from your letterhead on their trucks, so you'll want to design something flexible enough to be adapted to this or other uses.
- What is your client's self-image, and what is their image within their indus-

try and with their customers? Do they like this image and want their stationery to further communicate it, or do they think they need a change? If they do want to retool their image, their letterhead is a good place to start.
- What is their competition doing, and how can they stand out from the crowd? Research their primary competitors, and get letterhead from them whenever possible to get an idea of the industry standard—whether you decide to buck the industry trends or follow them, you'll need to know what they are.
- How will they use the system? For instance, if the letterhead is likely to be photocopied or faxed, darker paper stock would be a poor choice. If they often mail large items, you may need to design a sticker in addition to, or maybe instead of, an envelope. Additionally, some heat-set processes—such as thermography or foil-stamping—could melt if fed through a laser printer, ruining your client's office equipment. When possible, try to get input from the people who will use the stationery on a daily basis, not just the CEO of the company.
- Who are their clients? Are their clients' tastes likely to be similar to or different from their own? If the latter is true, then you're actually designing for two different kinds of end user, the client and the recipient, and you'll need to have background information about both of them, and to keep them both in mind when designing.
- Do recipients of your client's business correspondence want to receive it, do they have a neutral attitude toward it, or do they have no idea who your client is? The importance of using an eyecatching envelope to grab recipients' attention will, for instance, be more important for a publicity department that uses its letterhead to issue press releases than it would be for a

college admissions office that uses it to notify students that they've been admitted.
- Will the system's components often be seen together, or will each part need to stand alone most of the time? Is any component more important than the others? (If you can only splurge on four-color printing on one element of a system, and your client uses his business cards far more often than his letterhead, then splurging on the business card would be the sensible choice.)

Getting a Concept

Now it's time to take what you've learned and translate it into a concept that satisfies your client's objectives. Turning all this raw data into a visual concept that communicates your client's business and personality is one of the most mysterious parts of the design process, and the hardest to teach, but here are a few questions that you can use to generate ideas if you find yourself stuck:

- Does the client have a name that can be translated into a visual? Is there any way the client's name and business can be graphically linked?
- Can you find a way to graphically link your client's initials with what your client does (as on page 127)?
- Can you use a visual pun—illustrating your client's product or service literally—to convey your client's business (as on page 123)?
- Can you actually use the letterhead itself to demonstrate your client's skills (as on page 119)?
- If your budget allows, can you use a die cut or embossing to convey what your client does (as on page 116)?
- Is a more abstract or decorative solution appropriate for your client? If so, can you pick up colors or patterns from the client's office in the letterhead (as on page 25)? Or might a classic, elegant solution, utilizing foil-stamping, engraving, or a watermark,

be more appropriate?

- Are there concepts related to your client's business that might better be communicated with words than pictures? If so, how will you convey these ideas typographically?
- Can you find a way to link your type conceptually to what your client does (e.g. using icing to spell out a pastry chef's name, using script for a wedding planner, or using typewriter type for a copywriter, as on page 62)?
- Are there any photographs or patterns linked to what your client does that can be ghosted on the letterhead, or printed on the back of the sheet to show through?
- Would a retro look suit your client (as on pages 87 and 88)?
- Can the business card be designed in a shape that is appropriate for your client's name or business?

This is obviously just a start; for more ways to generate design ideas, see *Creativity for Graphic Designers* by Mark Oldach (North Light Books, 1995).

The Elements of Letterhead Design

Now that you've got that great idea, you'll need to translate it into a design that works on many levels—graphically, conceptually, and practically. And while your options are more limited than if you were designing, say, a booklet, you still have more choices than you might realize. Following are the major elements you have to work with, as well as brief comments about how each element differs in letterhead design.

COLOR: You have many of the same options with color that you would have with any other project, with just a few important exceptions. Since letterhead has to be reprinted so often, you're more likely to be restricted to a cheaper one- or two-color print job than on other design projects. If you do have four-color printing to work with, you will probably have

to use uncoated paper stock—meaning your colors won't pop the way they would on coated stock, unless you can afford spot varnish too. And all-over dark colors are, of course, usually not desirable—it will be too hard to read the correspondence, and faxing and photocopying it will just exacerbate the problem.

Despite these limitations, you can still use color inventively to communicate your client's business, spirit, and image. If you're limited in the number of colors you can use and want a classic look, think beyond black ink to other neutrals—dark grey, brown, even dark green or red—that will give your system a classic feel equal

to that of black ink, but with less of a possibility of a desktop-published look. And consider using different-colored paper stocks for each component of the system, to add color to your design for no extra cost. Some paper even includes patterns or four-color accents, extending your options, but if you're considering going this route you may want to pick your paper before you start designing.

GRAPHICS: Most letterhead includes at least one graphic—the company's logo. Whole books have been written about designing logos, but the same basic rules apply as in letterhead design: try to convey your client's business, as well as

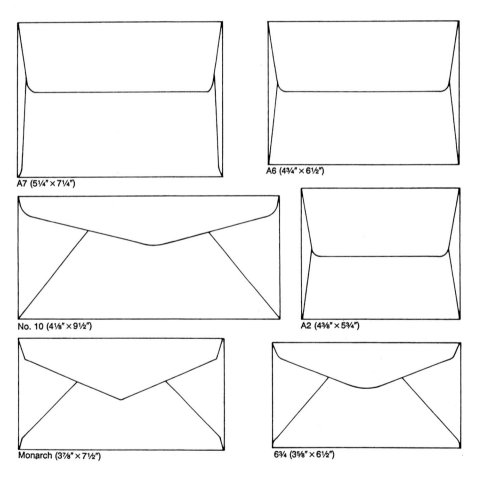

A7 (5¼" × 7¼")

A6 (4¾" × 6½")

No. 10 (4⅛" × 9½")

A2 (4⅜" × 5¾")

Monarch (3⅞" × 7½")

6¾ (3⅝" × 6½")

▲ Envelopes are either stock or converted. Stock envelopes are made and then printed; converted ones are printed then cut and folded. Stock envelopes are less expensive in small quantities and available with little lead time; however, they don't come in all paper grades.

You can have converted envelopes made from any paper, but it generally takes about four weeks. You'll also need to order about 25,000 to make envelope conversion a cost-effective option. The main reason for choosing an envelope conversion, however, is the printing technique to be used. Embossing, thermography and bleeds often do not work as well on stock envelopes.

some hint of their image or personality, as succinctly as possible.

Traditionally, letterhead design only had a few additional graphic possibilities beyond the logo—either the logo (or some detail of it) was enlarged and ghosted on the front of the first sheet, or the first sheet contained a watermark (either one that came with the paper, or one designed especially for the client). With the advent of stock photography, photo-manipulation, and clip art, it's now more common to see visuals used on letterhead strictly for decorative purposes. If planning additional visuals, however, keep your client's image in mind, and make sure there's still room enough to keep the piece functional—after all, letterhead is

meant to communicate a message.

Also, be especially careful when designing visuals for an envelope—if you're not tripped up by the limitations of various printing processes, you may be tripped up by the requirements of the post office. When in doubt, check with your printer, and with the U.S. Postal Service's "Domestic Mail Manual" (also known as Publication 25).

TYPE: Type is a crucial part of virtually any design, but it's especially important in letterhead and business card design—if you're giving your business card to someone, or if you're writing to them, you'll want them to know how to contact you, so readability is key. Even if your client is on the leading edge of their

industry, you should still be able to find a typeface that's both trendy and readable. Since you'll likely have little type on any of the pieces, you'll only be able to use a few typefaces (any more than three will probably look junky), so choosing typefaces that immediately communicate your client's personality is crucial.

PAPER: We've already discussed the color possibilities of paper; just as important in letterhead design is the texture of the paper you choose—unlike some other design pieces, your audience is guaranteed at some point to hold the letterhead or business card you designed, making its tactility an important component of the overall design. Thus, you should try to become sensitive to the differences between different types of paper weaves and weights, as well as differences that come from the content of the paper. In general, wove paper is smoother than laid paper, and paper with some cotton content is stiffer than paper without. To learn more about the qualities of different papers, get on the mailing lists of as many paper companies as you can, so you can receive their swatchbooks and promotions.

Another important consideration is whether to use recycled paper. You'll first need to ask your client whether they have a preference. If using recycled paper is important to them, you'll need to keep that in mind as you choose a stock for your job. Even if they don't have a preference, you might still want to use recycled paper—it's environmentally sound, and there are a wide variety of fine recycled stocks now available.

A final consideration is the opacity of the paper. If you want a design on the back of the letterhead to show through to the front, you'll need to check with your printer to make sure you choose the proper paper weight to achieve this effect. And while transparent vellum has become popular in letterhead design in recent years, as always make sure this will work with your client's office equipment.

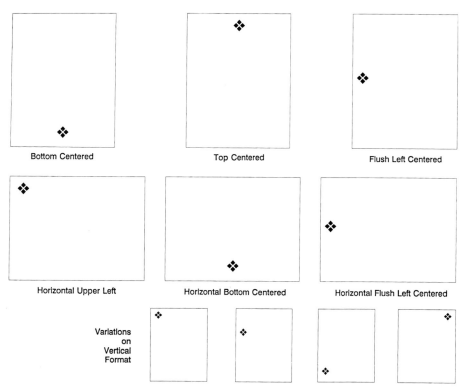

Bottom Centered   Top Centered   Flush Left Centered

Horizontal Upper Left   Horizontal Bottom Centered   Horizontal Flush Left Centered

Variations on Vertical Format

▲ **The traditional placement of the logo, company name and address is in the upper-left corner of the sheet, but you can, in fact, put them just about anywhere. Let your design suggest the placement. If you are doing a strongly symmetricial design, placing the information anywhere but the top center of the sheet may throw the design off entirely. However, a design that suggests motion might call for placement in the upper left or even in the upper right. Remember that the paper is to be typed and written on. Don't let your design get in the way of communication unless there is a compelling reason to do so.**

SIZE AND FORMAT: While you'll normally be working with a 8" x 11" letterhead sheet, a No. 10 (4 1/8" x 9") envelope, and a 2" x 3" business card, even within these limitations plenty of variety is possible. When laying out the letterhead, you have a lot of options on where to place the logo and text (see page 31). Also keep in mind that letterhead will almost always be seen first folded in thirds, so consider designing a two-sided layout that will look equally good whether the letterhead is folded or not (for an example of this, see page 120). If you use folds creatively (see page 64), you can also achieve some uniqueness within the rigid confines of business card design.

If your client (and their budget) will allow it, and if your client's office equipment can handle it, using a slightly larger or smaller size for any one of the letterhead components is guaranteed to make it stand out. Using a 6" x 9" envelope, so the letterhead can be folded into halves instead of thirds, is one possibility. Another is the use of a monarch size letterhead and envelope (which measure 7 1/4" x 10" and 3 7/8" x 8 7/8", respectively); this stationery size is traditionally associated with executive stationery, so it can be a good choice for a client who wants a prestigious feel.

PRINTING: Because of the subtlety and small scale of letterhead and business cards, special printing processes such as letterpress, engraving, thermography and the like are more important in this kind of design than any other—they're one of the best ways to set your client apart from the competition. We'll discuss printing options further in the last section of this introduction, but you'll need to decide which process or processes you want to use early on, and to discuss it with your printer in conjunction with the design you're planning, to make sure that what you're envisioning is actually possible in the real world. If you're planning to use more than one printing process,

Horizontal

Vertical

Short Fold Horizontal

Short Fold Vertical

"Z" Fold

Tent Fold

Gate Fold

Book Fold

▲ Business cards can be folded or unfolded. They can have a design or information printed on one side or both sides; the choices are virtually limitless. A business card, however, should be durable and easy to carry. Because cards are handled frequently, they should be printed on a heavy weight of paper, for example, 65# or 80# cover stock. Most business cards measure 3 1/2 x 2 inches, but through folds and die cuts, many kinds of cards may be produced. If the business card will be folded, have it scored on the press to ensure accuracy.

communication with your vendors will be especially important—if you try to emboss before you offset print your piece, for instance, your embossing will be flattened by the offset process.

Working With a Limited Budget

You've now examined all the ingredients that go into a letterhead system except for one—budget. Letterhead projects are often low-budget projects, but the ability to make the most of a limited budget in your design work will always stand you in good stead, even if you have more money to spend. With that in mind, here are questions you can ask yourself to make sure you're making the most of your budget, whether it's limited or less so:

- Have you considered creative ways you can combine offset and laser printing, to add an extra color for no extra cost?
- Can you use a different second color on each piece, to add a multi-colored look to your system for less?
- Have you considered using a variety of paper colors, to add color to a one- or two-color system (as on page 55)?
- Have you examined creative type and graphic layouts that will distract viewers from the lack of color variety?
- Can you tag some component of a one- or two-color system (for instance, the business card) onto a four-color print job, to allow you the luxury of four-color printing on at least one component of the piece? Or can you go in on a four-color press run with another firm (as on page 72)?
- Have you eliminated traps, bleeds, and other elements that will make your system more expensive to print (as on page 71)?
- Have you thought of using unusual sizes that could make your system attention-getting without spending more money?
- Have you simplified graphics so that they don't require high-quality printing (as on page 69)?
- Can you or your client do any kind of hand work on the system (such as folding, scoring, hole-punching or tying) that would add an additional element to the system for a little more work, but little more cost (as on pages 64 and 69)?
- Do you have any pre-existing dies that might work on this job? If you want to splurge on a custom die for this job, will it be something you might be able to use on a later job?
- Can you add additional graphics or colors with custom-designed rubber stamps?
- Is there any way you can strike a deal with the printer to have them print your job at a reduced cost, or free? If you're designing for a non-profit organization, you may be able to find a printer who believes in your client as much as you do; if it's your own letterhead, you may get a reduced cost if you do a lot of business with that printer, or if you offer to do some design work for the printer.

A Glossary of Printing Terms

Once you've translated your great concept for a letterhead system into a great design, you'll need to get it printed; here are the printing terms that are used most often in this book, and that you will need to understand if you're designing letterhead.

Converted Envelopes

Envelopes in which the paper stock is printed before the envelope is trimmed and glued; doing so allows you to use many printing methods—such as four-color process printing, printing inside the envelopes, embossing, bleeds, and die cuts—that would not be possible on stock envelopes. Converting envelopes is more expensive than using stock envelopes—the price will vary, depending upon which of the above printing methods you're using.

Debossing

Using a metal or plastic die to press letters or illustrations into paper, creating a depressed image (the opposite of embossing).

Die Cutting

Cutting special shapes into a piece of paper using a formed, metal-edged die. Usually a thicker paper must be used, as thinner stocks are likely to get torn during this process. If a printing job requires a custom-made or complex die cut, the cost of your print job will increase; if you can use the die again (you will get to keep it), it could be worth the extra cost.

Double Hit or Bump

To increase the intensity of a color by printing it twice. The cost for a double hit of one color is approximately that of a two-color job, but it may be worth it if you're going for a really dramatic look.

Embossing

Using a metal or plastic die to press letters or illustrations into paper, creating a raised, three-dimensional image. Several effects may be achieved through embossing: images or edges may be beveled, multilevel, three-dimensional or sculpted. When embossing, specify a heavyweight, strong paper with longer fiber formation, and keep in mind that with deeper impressions, more space must be allowed between design elements for proper shaping of the paper. Blind embossing, a process in which no color or foil is added to the raised surface, produces a classic bas-relief effect, and appears smaller than designed once it is printed.

Engraving

A printing process using etched or recessed plates. The recessed plates are filled with ink, and as the printing press exerts force on the paper, the paper is pushed into the recesses and ink, creating a raised image on one side of the page and indentations on the other. Engraving is ideal for small type, as it produces fine, precise lines. When planning a design to be engraved, remember that deeper etches are possible on heavier paper (20 to 24 pounds is best), and that the smaller the type or more intricate the artwork, the less depth can be etched. As most engraving plates are 5 x 8 inches, letterheads with engraved images at the top and bottom may need two press runs, adding to the cost of the job. Though engraved plates cost more than other types of printing plates, they are durable and may be used to print both letters and business cards, lowering the overall cost of producing a letterhead system.

Kraft paper

A strong, unbleached paper manufactured using kraft pulp. In the kraft pulping process, fiber is separated from lignin—the glue-like substance that holds together the cellulose fibers of wood plants—by cooking woodchips with steam and pressure.

Letterpress

A relief printing method using cast metal type or plates, in which the areas to be printed are raised above the nonprinting areas and ink rollers only touch the raised areas. The inked type or plates are then pressed into the paper, often leaving a depression where the type or plate hits the paper. Often used as a cheaper alternative to embossing or engraving.

Offset printing

An indirect printing process in which ink is transferred to paper from a blanket that carries an impression from the printing plate, rather than directly from the plate itself; this is the most common printing method.

Thermography

A type of finish applied after printing that creates the raised effect of engraved printing with less cost and time involved. In the thermography process, special ink is used during offset printing; then, a resinous powder is applied to the paper, and the paper is passed through a heater. In the heater, the powder fuses to the ink and swells, creating the raised image. The powder on the unprinted areas of the paper is then vacuumed off. When using thermography, specify paper with a basis weight of 20 pounds or more; type as small as four point may be thermographed, but don't use intricate detail and large, solid areas on the same sheet—two separate resins are required, and the resin used for fine lines may produce an uneven, mottled effect in the solid areas. Since this is a heat-set process, it often cannot be used in photocopiers or laser printers—the resinous powder may melt—and for this reason has fallen out of favor in the 1990s (there are few, if any, examples in this edition of this book). It may still be an appropriate choice for business cards, or for clients who type or handwrite their correspondence.

Varnish

A coating which is printed on top of a printed sheet to protect it from scratches, to add a glossy finish, or to add a bit of color. Certain areas of a page may be spot-varnished to attract attention and add emphasis to a design, photograph, or bit of text; spot-varnishing is comparable in cost to a two-color job. Varnish works best when applied to coated paper. To make a surface look smooth and clear, use a gloss varnish; to make it look soft, use a dull varnish. Check with your printer if you are unsure how a varnish will work with your design plans.

Visual
Effect

Think of the official letterheads you've received in the mail throughout your lifetime, and a blur of black or gray addresses and phone numbers—maybe with a few tired logos, if you're lucky—will probably pass before your eyes.

If any individual example actually sticks out in your mind, it's probably due to a great visual effect—an offbeat illustration, a uniquely printed envelope, a beautiful color combination. You'll find plenty of examples of great visual effects in this chapter—examples that may stay in your mind long after you close this book. Sure, you may be able to get away with designing a letterhead for a client with a simple type treatment and nothing else, but will the recipient of the letter remember your client? And when it comes time for another design job, will your client remember you?

The future of telecommunications never looked so good.

[F U T U R E C O M ™]

Jones Intercable, Inc.

617-A South Pickett Street

Alexandria, VA 22304

(703) 823-3000

Fax: (703) 823-3061

Art Director/Studio Steve Wedeen/
Vaughn/Wedeen Creative
Designers/Studio Dan Flynn, Steve
Wedeen/Vaughn/Wedeen Creative
Photographer Stephen Marks
Client/Service Jones Intercable/tele-
phone service for cable company
Paper Neenah Classic Crest Avon
Brilliant White
Type Garamond Italic, Franklin
Gothic
Colors Three, black and match
Printing Offset
Software QuarkXPress, Adobe
Photoshop

Concept To suggest the business of
this start-up company without lock-
ing it into a traditional logo, the
designers decided on a television/
phone image that suggested the
client's business without hindering
their positioning (or possible reposi-
tioning) in the market.
Special Production Techniques Since
the designers weren't able to find a
satisfactory stock photograph, they
commissioned a local photographer
to achieve the look they wanted.
Initial Print Run 1,000

Alexandria, VA 22304

617-A South Pickett Street

Jones Intercable, Inc.

[F U T U R E C O M ™]

*The future of telecommunications
never looked so good.*

Art Director/Studio Carlos Segura/
Segura Inc.
Designer/Studio Carlos Segura/
Segura Inc.
Illustrator Tony Klassen
Client/Service XXX
Snowboards/snowboards
Paper Fox River Confetti
Type Amplifier
Colors Four, process
Printing Offset
Software QuarkXPress, Adobe
Photoshop, Adobe Illustrator

Concept Snowboard companies are
known for their interest in cutting-
edge graphics, and this set of business cards for XXX Snowboards fol-
lows in this tradition of nontradition.
Special Visual Effects Each person at
the company has a unique graphic
treatment on the back of his or her
card.
Initial Print Run 3,000

XXX Snowboards

Jim Spinello

42 Sherwood Terrace, Suite Number 2
Lake Bluff, Illinois 60044
708.735.9493 t   708.735.9805 f

GLEN S. GARLAND
42 Sherwood Terrace, Suite Number 2
Lake Bluff, Illinois 60044
708.735.9493 t   708.735.9805 f

XXX Snowboards

4712 W. Moorhead Circle. Boulder, CO   303.499.7950 tel   303.499.1750

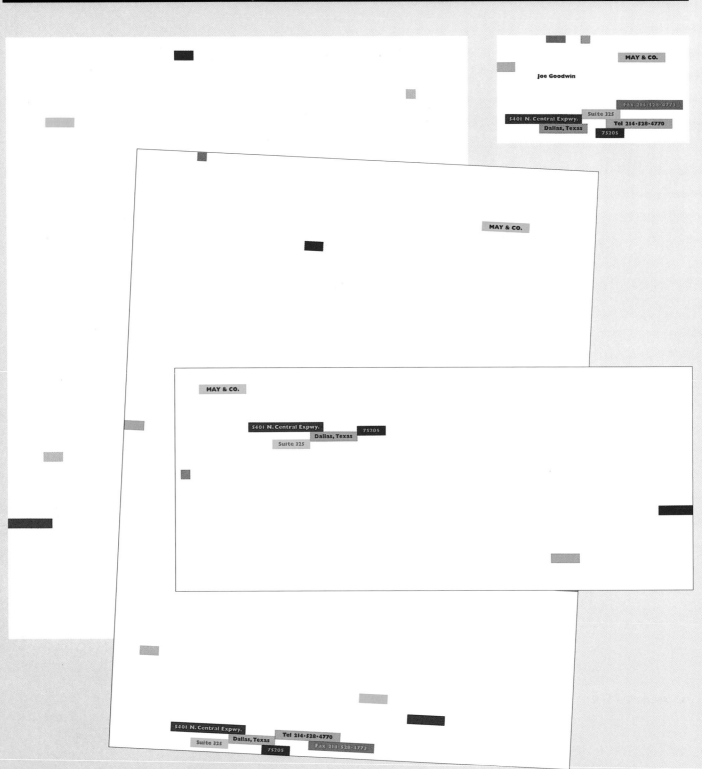

Art Director/Studio Douglas May/
May & Co.
Designer/Studio Jo Ortiz/May & Co.
Client/Service May & Co./corporate
graphic design
Paper Simpson Starwhite Vicksburg
Type Gill Sans Bold

Colors Six, match
Printing Offset
Software QuarkXPress
Billable Hours to Complete 36

Concept This colorful, attention-
getting system for a design firm com-

municates the integrated nature of the
design firm's approach to problem
solving.
Special Visual Effects The elements
of the system, which at first glance
seem to be randomly placed, actually
serve as placement guides for ele-

ments within correspondence, ensur-
ing the consistency of type placement.
Cost $7,500
Initial Print Run 5,000 (letterhead,
envelope); 2,500 (disk label, mailing
label, second sheet); 500 each of 9
names (business card)

Art Directors/Studio Mark Schwartz,
Joyce Nesnadny/Nesnadny +
Schwartz
Designers/Studio Mark Schwartz,
Joyce Nesnadny, Michelle
Moehler/Nesnadny + Schwartz
Photographers Various
Client/Service Rock and Roll Hall
of Fame + Museum/museum
Paper Strathmore Elements
Type Century
Colors Two over two, match
Printing Offset
Software QuarkXPress, Adobe
Photoshop

Concept The front is
conservative enough to
give this system for the Rock and Roll Hall
of Fame + Museum the prestigious look it
requires, but the back uses lively photography
from the museum's collection to give the
system the spirit of fun it also needs.
Special Visual Effects The system amply
utilizes photographs from the Rock and Roll
Hall of Fame's collection, but restricts the
reproduction of those images to two different
duotones, giving the system visual coherence.
Initial Press Run Various

Art Director/Studio Dan Flynn/
Vaughn/Wedeen Creative
Designer/Studio Dan Flynn/
Vaughn/Wedeen Creative
Photographer Stephen Marks
Client/Product Motorola/computer
chips
Paper Neenah Classic Crest Solar
White Writing
Type Copperplate, VWC house face
Colors Four, process
Printing Offset
Software QuarkXPress, Adobe
Photoshop

Concept In this system for Compass,
a management program within
Motorola, the designers used a row
of compass visuals that look more
like illustrations than the photographs they actually are. The different styles of compasses depicted
represent the diversity of groups
receiving the letterhead; the subtlety
of the images, as well as the corporate nature of the system's color
scheme, gives the letterhead a professional feel.
Initial Print Run 20,000

C O M P A S S

CHARTING OUR MANAGEMENT/PROFESSIONAL ABILITIES STEP BY STEP

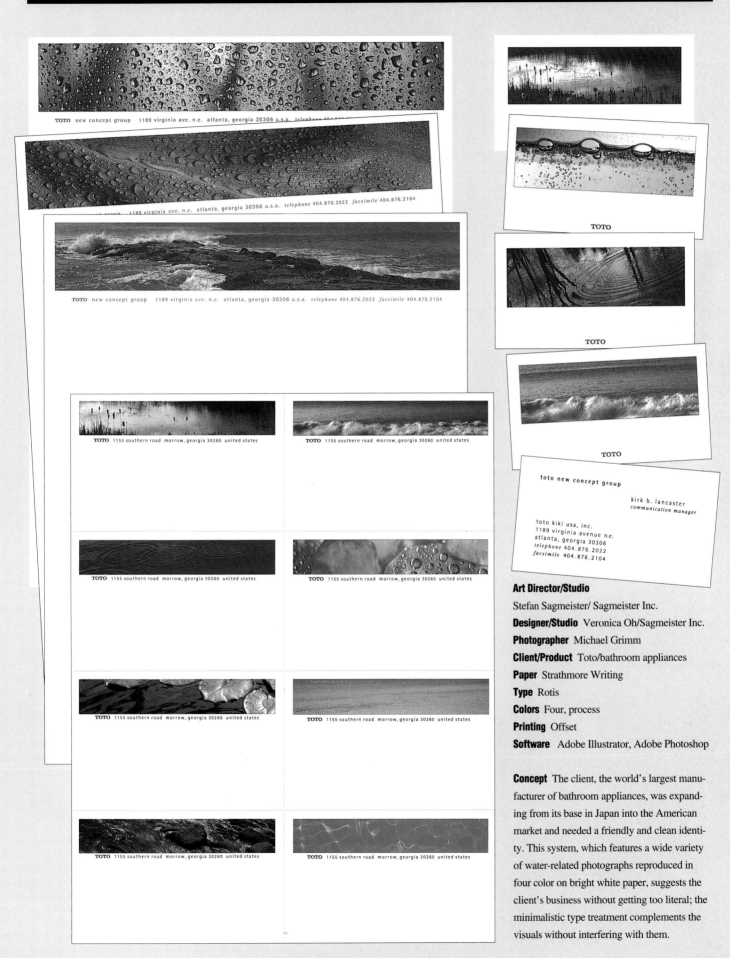

Art Director/Studio
Stefan Sagmeister/ Sagmeister Inc.
Designer/Studio Veronica Oh/Sagmeister Inc.
Photographer Michael Grimm
Client/Product Toto/bathroom appliances
Paper Strathmore Writing
Type Rotis
Colors Four, process
Printing Offset
Software Adobe Illustrator, Adobe Photoshop

Concept The client, the world's largest manufacturer of bathroom appliances, was expanding from its base in Japan into the American market and needed a friendly and clean identity. This system, which features a wide variety of water-related photographs reproduced in four color on bright white paper, suggests the client's business without getting too literal; the minimalistic type treatment complements the visuals without interfering with them.

Art Directors/Studio Bradford Lawton, Jennifer Griffith/The Bradford Lawton Design Group
Designer/Studio Bradford Lawton/The Bradford Lawton Design Group
Illustrator Mark Weakley
Client/Service Southwest Texas State University/university
Paper Strathmore Writing Natural White Wove, Strathmore Text Wove Natural White
Type Times, Times Roman, Copperplate Thirty AB
Colors Four, process
Printing Offset
Software Adobe Illustrator, QuarkXPress
Billable Hours to Complete 64

Concept The client's centennial campaign was developed to raise funds from university alumni over a five-year period. This nostalgic system for the campaign—prominently featuring the campus's main landmark, Old Main, in a stamplike format—is a sophisticated solution that encourages alumni to reminisce fondly about their time spent at Southwest Texas State University.
Initial Print Run 20,000

601 University Drive • San Marcos TX 78666-4612 • (512) 245-2396 • Fax (512) 245-3817 • Member, Texas State University System

Art Director/Studio Patricia Belyea/
Belyea Design Alliance

Designers/Studio Adrianna Jumping
Eagle, Samantha Hunt/Belyea
Design Alliance

Illustrators Jani Drewfs, Brian
O'Neill

Client/Service Belyea Design
Alliance/graphic design

Paper Simpson Protocol

Type Bodega Sans

Colors Four, process, with process
yellow replaced with match

Printing Offset

Software Aldus FreeHand, Painter,
Adobe Photoshop, QuarkXPress

Billable Hours to Complete 90

Concept The use of a vibrant graphic gives this stationery system for a
design firm a distinct personality.
The match yellow used throughout
the system has become a signature
color for the firm and is now used on
the walls and other objects in the
office.

Cost-Cutting Techniques The system was run through a two-color
press twice. Stickers of the four-
color graphic element liven up the
envelope and other components of
the system without adding cost.

Initial Print Run 1,000

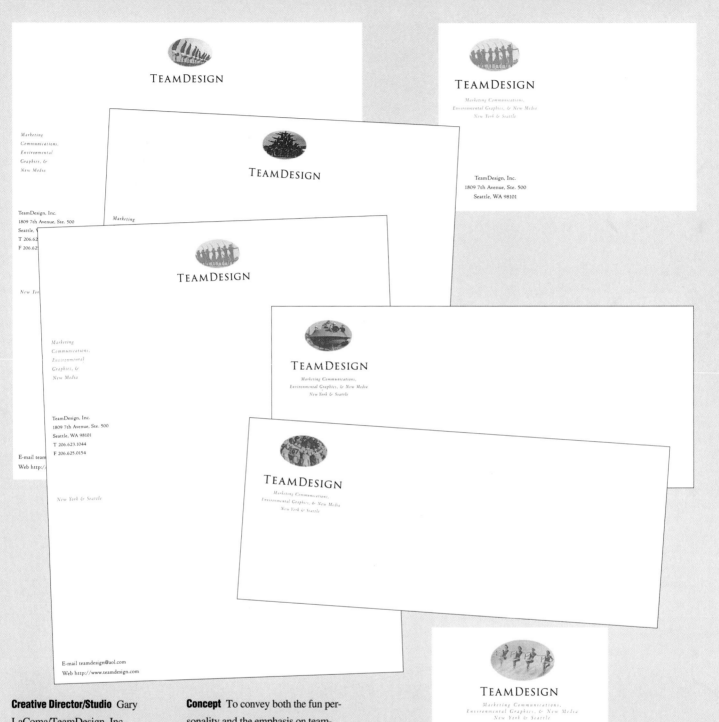

Creative Director/Studio Gary LaComa/TeamDesign, Inc.
Designer/Studio Ross Hogin/TeamDesign, Inc.
Photographer Stock
Client/Service TeamDesign, Inc./graphic design
Paper Strathmore Writing
Type Trajan (logotype), Centaur
Colors Two, black and match
Printing Offset
Software Aldus PageMaker, Aldus FreeHand

Concept To convey both the fun personality and the emphasis on teamwork in this design firm, a variety of stock photographs humorously depicting different kinds of teams is used as the visual centerpiece of this system.
Cost-Cutting Techniques A different match color is used as the second color on each piece of the system, giving it a lively look at a reasonable cost.
Initial Print Run 5,000

Art Director/Studio Fani Chung/Gee + Chung Design
Designer/Studio Fani Chung/Gee + Chung Design
Illustrator Fani Chung
Client/Service Community Partnership of Santa Clara County/ nonprofit organization dedicated to building healthy communities
Paper French Speckletone Cream
Type Bodoni (logotype), Bodoni Italic (address), Copperplate 33BC (mission statement)
Colors Two, match, on each piece
Printing Offset
Software QuarkXPress, Adobe Illustrator
Billable Hours to Complete 30

Concept This system conveys the client's mission—the building of healthy communities—visually, with the use of hands reaching for the stars and working together, and verbally, with the incorporation of the client's mission statement on the stationery.
Special Production Techniques The die-cut business card utilizes a hand-drawn wavy edge, providing another human touch to the design.
Cost-Cutting Techniques Each component of the system uses a different second color, providing the cumulative effect of a multicolor system at a reasonable cost.
Initial Print Run 15,000

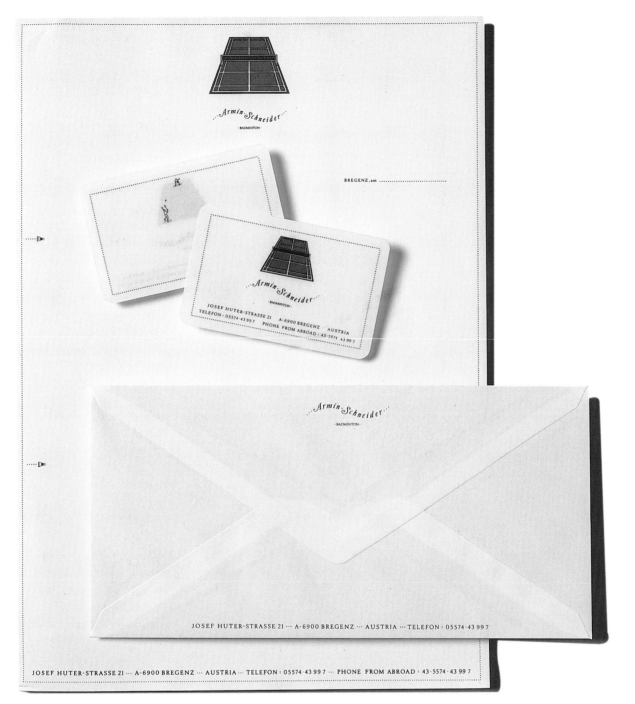

Art Director/Studio Stefan Sagmeister/Sagmeister Inc.

Designer/Studio Stefan Sagmeister/ Sagmeister Inc.

Illustrator Stefan Sagmeister

Client/Product Armin Schneider/ badminton

Paper Strathmore Writing

Type Bembo

Colors Two, match

Printing Offset plus lamination (business card)

Concept This system playfully conveys the client's business—badminton—with illustrations and icons that all refer to the game. The designer capitalized on the transparency of the paper by having the illustration of a badminton court on the front of the letterhead and business card and having the players printed only on the back, revealing the total picture of the players on the court only when the system is backlit.

Special Production Techniques The business card was printed on the same sheet as the letterhead and then laminated (a cheap process in Austria).

Initial Print Run 1,000

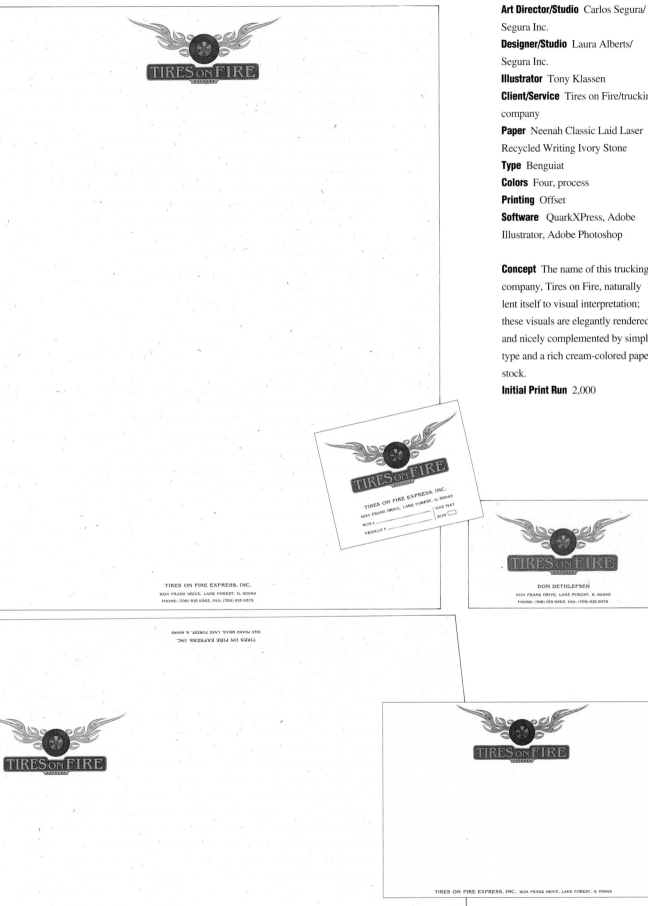

Art Director/Studio Carlos Segura/
Segura Inc.
Designer/Studio Laura Alberts/
Segura Inc.
Illustrator Tony Klassen
Client/Service Tires on Fire/trucking
company
Paper Neenah Classic Laid Laser
Recycled Writing Ivory Stone
Type Benguiat
Colors Four, process
Printing Offset
Software QuarkXPress, Adobe
Illustrator, Adobe Photoshop

Concept The name of this trucking
company, Tires on Fire, naturally
lent itself to visual interpretation;
these visuals are elegantly rendered,
and nicely complemented by simple
type and a rich cream-colored paper
stock.
Initial Print Run 2,000

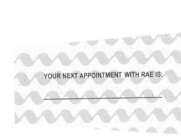

Art Director/Studio Daniel Fortin,
George Fok/Tarzan Communications
Inc.
Designer/Studio Daniel Fortin,
George Fok/Tarzan Communications
Inc.
Client/Service Enzyme Digital
Marketing/three-dimensional anima-
tion and video game development
Paper Cornwall Coated
Type Stealth, Meta
Colors Two, match
Printing Offset

Concept A futuristic typeface over-
laying an organic visual is an intriguing solution for this business card for
a client with a technology-oriented
business—animation and video
game development—and an organic
name—Enzyme.
Special Production Techniques A
wavy die-cut edge complements the
card's central visual.
Special Visual Effects Flipping the
"e" for the second "e" in the word
enzyme is a clever touch that
enhances the symmetry of the logotype, as well as adding to its futuristic look.
Initial Print Run 1,000

Art Director/Studio Rick Eiber/Rick
Eiber Design (RED)
Designer/Studio Rick Eiber/Rick
Eiber Design (RED)
Illustrator Richard Kehl
Client/Service Richard Kehl/illustra-
tion
Paper Springhill CIS
Type Univers
Colors Four, process
Printing Offset

Concept This business card for an
illustrator lets his work speak for
itself. The card is folded in such a
way that it folds down for easy storage in a wallet or Rolodex but can
also be freestanding for display; the

middle panel provides room for the
artist to write a note in metallic ink
when gift-giving.
Cost-Cutting Techniques The card
was tagged onto a four-color form
that included notecards and book-
marks by the illustrator, printed one
side only.
Cost $650 (production only; printing
and design traded)
Initial Print Run 3,000

Art Director/Studio John
Sayles/Sayles Graphic Design
Designer/Studio Jennifer
Elliott/Sayles Graphic Design
Illustrator Jennifer Elliott
Client/Service Rae Simonini
Hildreth/hair designer and nail
technician
Paper Hopper Nekoosa Feltweave
Parchment
Type Helvetica
Colors One, match
Printing Offset

Concept The diagonal cut of this
business card still fits the traditional
card holder but gives this piece for a
nail technician/hair designer a clean
edge and a smooth look. Elements of
the logo are screened on the back of
the card for a textured look.
Cost-Cutting Techniques While the
card originally appears die-cut, a
closer look reveals that angled
straight cuts were used instead. Only
one ink color was used.
Initial Print Run 1,500

Art Director/Studio Petrula Vrontikis/Vrontikis Design Office

Designer/Studio Kim Sage (stationery), Lorna Stovall (logo)/Vrontikis Design Office

Client/Service Global Investment Concept, Inc./restaurant

Paper Neenah Classic Crest

Type Hand-lettering (logo), Veljovic (address)

Colors Three, match, with metallic and varnish

Printing Offset

Billable Hours to Complete 40

Concept This elegant system reflects the opulence of the restaurant for which it was designed. Contrast between the exuberant script of the hand-lettered logo and the classic text copy and between the pared-down visuals on the front of the system and the wild colors and patterns on the back maintains the viewer's interest.

Special Production Techniques The back of the letterhead features varnish and full-bleed patterns.

Special Visual Effects The placement of rules and body copy on both the letterhead and envelope is an unusual take on traditional design elements.

Initial Print Run 5,000

"Home-grown reading is Love."
215 Briarhill Drive, Mississauga, Ontario L5G 2N4 Tel: 905-274-5628

"Home-grown reading is Love."
215 Briarhill Drive, Mississauga, Ontario L5G 2N4

Art Director/Studio Ric Riordon/The
Riordon Design Group Inc.
Designer/Studio Don Wheaton/The
Riordon Design Group Inc.
Client/Service Baby
Bookworms/preschool reading
education
Paper Concerto
Type Garamond
Colors Three, match
Printing Offset
Software Adobe Illustrator,
QuarkXPress
Billable Hours to Complete 30

Concept The quaint illustration style
and typeface used in this system are
appropriate for the client, who specializes in teaching preschool children to read. The illustration even
suggests the client's method of
education—photo-phonetics.
Visual Special Effects The logo for
the system is enlarged and ghosted as
a background image on the letterhead.
Cost $3,500
Initial Print Run 1,000 (letterhead,
envelope); 500 (business card)

Art Director/Studio Mike Salisbury/ Mike Salisbury Communications
Designer/Studio Mary Evelyn McCough/Mike Salisbury Communications
Client/Service The Village/state-of-the-art recording studio
Paper Strathmore Writing Wove Bright White
Type Radiant, Franklin Gothic
Colors Three, black and match
Printing Offset
Software Adobe Illustrator, QuarkXPress

Concept To capitalize upon the most noteworthy feature of this recording studio, this system uses as its visual motif the studio's famous green door.
Special Visual Effects The foldout business card is consistent with the theme of the system and interactive (a quality the client had asked for).
Cost Printing only (design was traded out)
Initial Print Run 1,000

Art Director/Studio Rick Vaughn/
Vaughn/Wedeen Studio
Designer/Studio Rick Vaughn/
Vaughn/Wedeen Studio
Illustrator Rick Vaughn
Client/Service Duke City Marathon/
annual marathon
Paper Neenah Classic Crest
Type Courier
Colors Three, black and match
Printing Offset
Software QuarkXPress, Aldus
FreeHand

Concept The Duke City Marathon is
held annually in Albuquerque. For
the tenth anniversary of the event,
the organizers commissioned this
redesign of the marathon's logo and
stationery. The logo and accompany-
ing graphic elements cleverly suggest both the nature of the event and
its location with running figures that
are takeoffs on ancient rock art found
in Albuquerque's Petroglyphs.
Special Visual Effects A whimsical
border of running figures enlivens
both the letterhead and the envelope
flap. With a vibrant color scheme of
gold, red and black, the designers
avoided the Southwestern color
motif that would have been a more
expected—and more clichéd—
choice.

PO Box 4543

Albuquerque

New Mexico

87196-4543

telephone

505-890-1018

facsimile

505-898-3084

PO Box 4543

Albuquerque

New Mexico

87196-4543

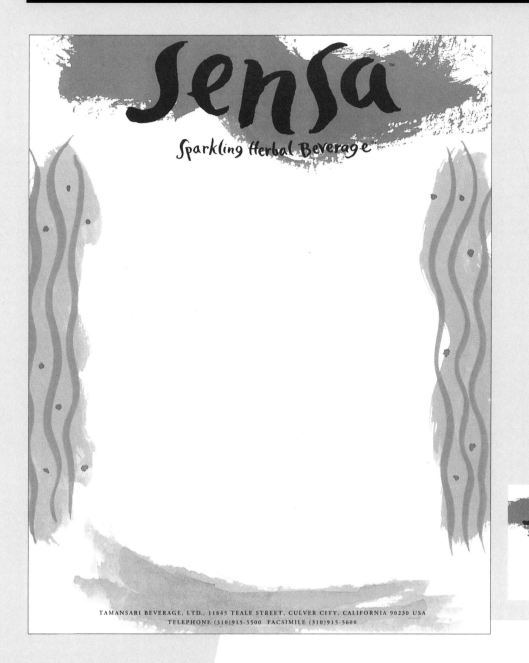

Art Director/Studio Rod Dyer/
Dyer/Mutchnick Group, Inc.
Designer/Studio John Sabel/
Dyer/Mutchnick Group, Inc.
Illustrator John Sabel
Client/Product Tamansari Beverage/
herbal beverages
Paper Neenah Environment White
Wove
Type Adobe Garamond
Colors Four, process
Printing Offset
Software QuarkXPress, Adobe
Photoshop

Concept A combination of watercol-
or and acrylic painting, dynamically
colored and exuberantly rendered,
conveys the freshness and clarity of
the client's product—herbal beverages.
Cost $15,000
Initial Print Run 2,500

Our Lady of Lourdes
REHABILITATION HOSPITAL

1151 N. Rock Road • Wichita, KS 67206 • Tel 316-634-3400 • Fax 316-634-1141

Our Lady of Lourdes
REHABILITATION HOSPITAL
1151 N. Rock Road • Wichita, KS 67206

Art Directors/Studio Sonia Greteman,
Todd Gimlin/Greteman Group
Client/Service Our Lady of Lourdes/
rehabilitation hospital
Paper Neenah Classic Crest
Columns Natural
Type Berkeley
Colors Two, match
Printing Offset
Software Aldus FreeHand
Billable Hours to Complete 10

Concept This system visually references the healing waters associated
with the hospital's namesake to convey the concepts of healing, prayer
and hope appropriate to the hospital's mission.
Budget $3,000
Initial Print Run 5,000

Our Lady of
Lourdes

REHABILITATION
HOSPITAL

KIM OLDS
Administrative Assistant
Medical Staff Coordinator

1151 N. Rock Road
Wichita, KS 67206
Tel 316-634-3447
Fax 316-634-1141

Art Director/Studio Petrula Vrontikis/Vrontikis Design Office
Designers/Studio Christina Hsiao (logo), Carrie Dobbel (stationery)/Vrontikis Design Office
Client/Service The Georgian Hotel/hotel
Paper Neenah Classic Crest
Type Dolmen (logo), Gill Sans (address)
Colors Two, match
Printing Offset
Software QuarkXPress, Adobe Photoshop, Adobe Illustrator
Billable Hours to Complete 25

Concept To convey the primary appeal of the hotel—a quaint, inviting and historic place with an ocean location—the designers came up with this attractive and relaxed solution.
Special Visual Effects A detail of the swirling ocean in the logo is ghosted and used as a background texture on every component of the system.
Cost $5,000
Initial Print Run 25

THE
GEORGIAN

1415 Ocean Avenue
Santa Monica, California
90401

Santa Monica's gracious hotel by the sea.

THE
GEORGIAN

1415 Ocean Avenue

Santa Monica, California 90401

Telephone 310.395.9945

Facsimile 310.451.3374

Santa Monica's gracious hotel by the sea.

THE
GEORGIAN

1415 Ocean Avenue
Santa Monica, California 90401
Telephone 310.395.9945
Facsimile 310.451.3374

Santa Monica's gracious hotel by the sea.

Art Director/Studio Mark Sackett/
Sackett Design Associates
Designers/Studio Mark Sackett,
Wayne Sakamoto/Sackett Design
Associates
Illustrators Wayne Sakamoto, James
Sakamoto
Client/Service Harvest
Market/organic market
Paper Neenah Terrazzo Wove
Type Courier (hand-manipulated)
Colors One, black
Printing Offset
Billable Hours to Complete 40

Concept This rustic system for an
organic market conveys the handcrafted feel the client wanted.
Keeping the colors and graphics simple gives the system an appropriately
down-to-earth feel.
Special Visual Effects Art and
typography were manipulated to
achieve a weathered look.
Cost $4,000
Initial Print Run 1,000

Designers Jeff Fabian, Laura
Latham, Mimi Massé, Scott Pollard,
Michael Shea, Sam Shelton
Photographer Annie Adjanavich
Client/Service Design Industries
Foundation Fighting AIDS/AIDS
fund-raising organization
Paper Cougar Opaque Text
Type Helvetica
Colors Four, black and match
Printing Offset

Concept This letterhead for DIFFA,
an AIDS charity organization, projects a soft and artistic image appropriate for the organization and for its
goals.
Special Visual Effects The use of
ghosted photography gives the letterhead a fine-art appearance that suits
the design-related nature of the organization.
Cost All services donated
Initial Print Run 3,000 each piece

Art Director/Studio Steve Wedeen/
Vaughn/Wedeen Creative
Designer/Studio Steve Wedeen/
Vaughn/Wedeen Creative
Photographer Stock
Client/Service Jones Computer
Network/computer information
channel
Paper Weyerhaeuser Cougar
Opaque Smooth Offset
Type Univers Black
Colors Four, process
Printing Offset
Software QuarkXPress, Adobe
Photoshop

Concept To illustrate the variety of
information available on the Jones
Computer Network Channel, the
designer computer-manipulated and
layered stock photographs.
Initial Print Run 30,000

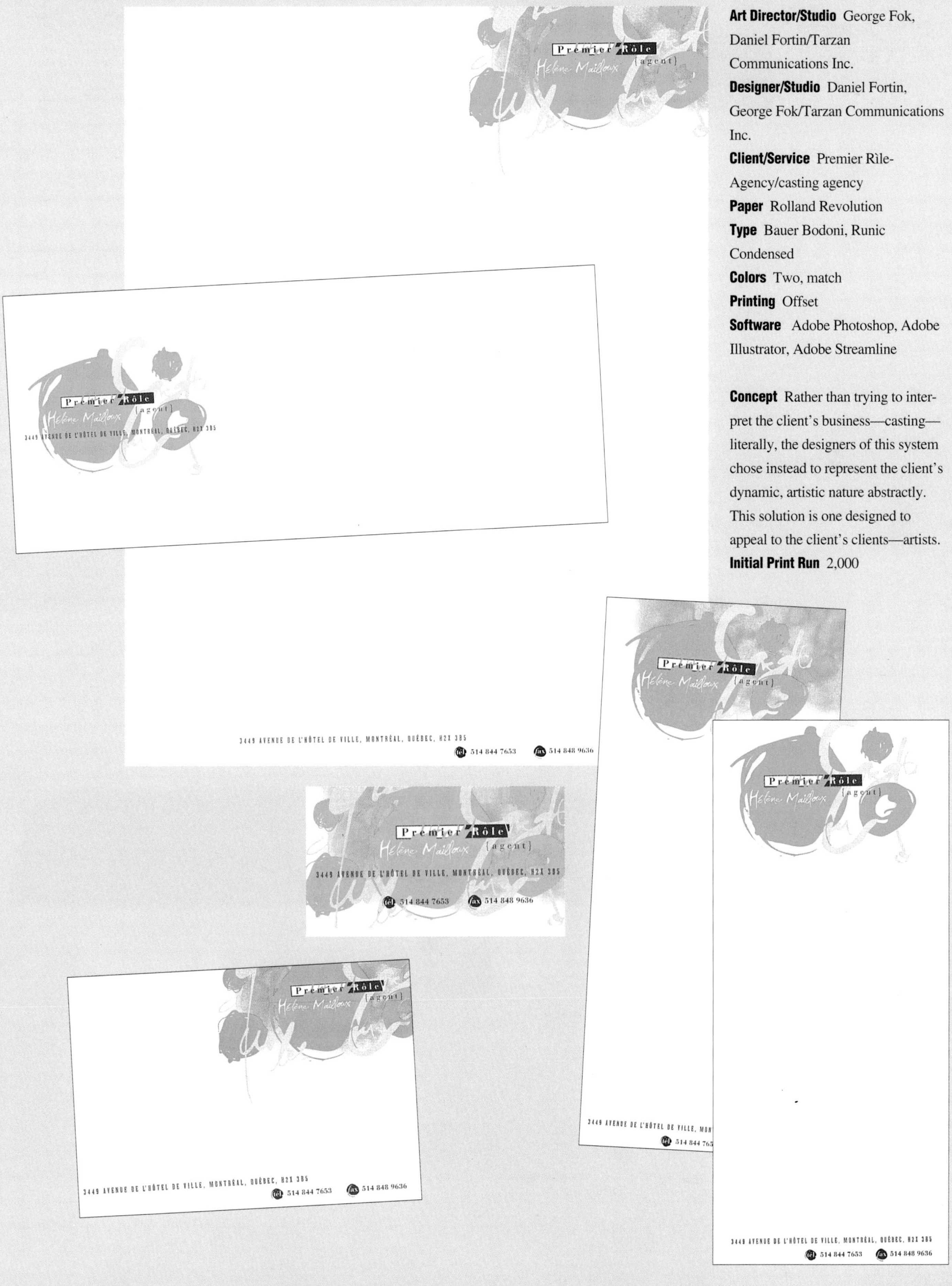

Art Director/Studio George Fok, Daniel Fortin/Tarzan Communications Inc.

Designer/Studio Daniel Fortin, George Fok/Tarzan Communications Inc.

Client/Service Premier Rìle-Agency/casting agency

Paper Rolland Revolution

Type Bauer Bodoni, Runic Condensed

Colors Two, match

Printing Offset

Software Adobe Photoshop, Adobe Illustrator, Adobe Streamline

Concept Rather than trying to interpret the client's business—casting—literally, the designers of this system chose instead to represent the client's dynamic, artistic nature abstractly. This solution is one designed to appeal to the client's clients—artists.

Initial Print Run 2,000

Art Director/Studio Jack Anderson/ Hornall Anderson Design Works

Designers/Studio Jack Anderson, Julie Keenan/Hornall Anderson Design Works

Client/Service GE Capital Assurance/annuities company

Paper Weyerhaeuser Cougar Opaque Offset

Type Univers Condensed, DF Organics

Colors Four, match

Printing Offset

Software Aldus FreeHand

Concept The sun is used throughout as a motif in this stationery for a corporate retreat in Hawaii. Combining this carefree illustration with a warm yet sophisticated color scheme makes the retreat look both fun and professional.

Cost-Cutting Techniques The sun illustration was stock art.

Art Director/Studio Brian Hawkins/
Pierson Hawkins Inc. Advertising
Designers/Studio Michael Besch,
Chip Hisle/Pierson Hawkins Inc.
Advertising
Photographer Brian Mark
Client/Service Pierson Hawkins Inc.
Advertising/advertising
Type PH Book
Colors Six, match and process
Printing Offset
Software QuarkXPress, Adobe
Photoshop, Adobe Illustrator
Billable Hours to Complete 100

Concept This system for an advertising firm uses a gyroscope motif to
reference the firm's self-description:
"strategically guided imagination."
This motif is flexible enough to be
used on its own elsewhere; it even
allows the firm to give away gyro-
scopes as a premium.
Special Visual Effects The rounded
side flaps on the envelopes give the
system an extra touch.

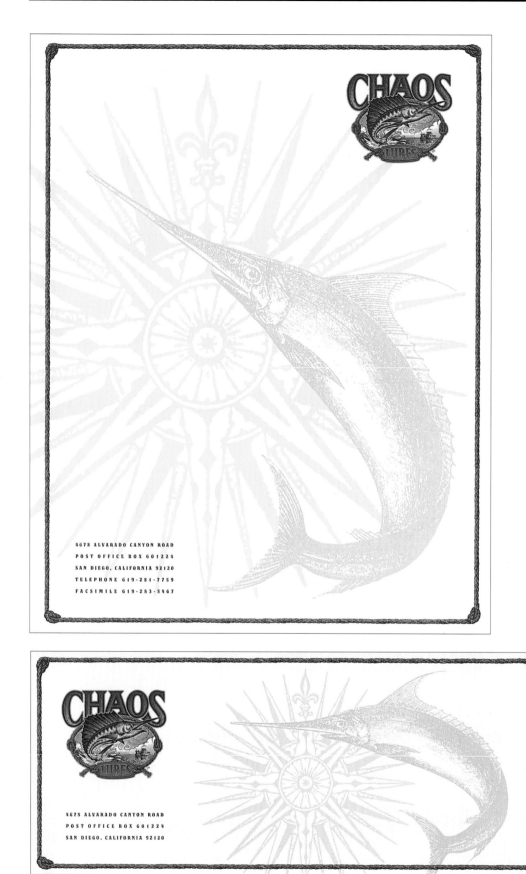

Art Director/Studio José Serrano/
Mires Design, Inc.
Designer/Studio José Serrano/Mires
Design, Inc.
Illustrator Tracy Sabin
Client/Product Chaos/deep-sea
fishing lures
Paper Simpson Starwhite Vicksburg
Cream
Type Negro Plain
Colors Four, process
Printing Offset
Software Adobe Illustrator,
QuarkXPress
Billable Hours to Complete 54
(logo), 50 (identity system)

Concept To give this start-up company the credibility of a company
that has been in business a long time,
the designer used a traditional layout
and an old-fashioned illustration
style to give the system an old-world
feel.
Special Production Techniques An
engraved look was simulated on the
logo, with the help of a feature in
Adobe Illustrator.
Initial Print Run 2,000

PACIFIC COAST FEATHER COMPANY • 1964 FOURTH AVE. S. • BOX 80385 • SEATTLE, WASHINGTON • 98108 • USA

JOE CRAWFORD
GENERAL MANANGER
FEATHER & DOWN PROCESSING

LOCAL: (206)653-3696
SEATTLE: (206)743-1677
FAX: (206)659-4222

14524 40TH AVE. NE
MARYSVILLE, WA 98270-8903 USA

Art Director/Studio Jack Anderson/
Hornall Anderson Design Works

Designers/Studio Jack Anderson,
Julie Lock, Heidi Favour, Leo
Raymundo/Hornall Anderson
Design Works

Illustrator Carolyn Vibbert

Client/Service Pacific Coast Feather
Company/manufacturer of pillows
and down comforters

Paper Crane Crest

Type Copperplate

Colors Four, process

Printing Offset

Software Aldus FreeHand, Adobe
Photoshop

Concept The objective: to retain
some previous elements of the
client's identity (specifically the oval
motif and the goose) while adding
warmth to the identity. The solution:
an illustrative logo that suggests the
client's Northwest location with the
use of mountains, trees and water
rendered in a warm color scheme.

Special Visual Effects A small leaf
icon is used consistently throughout
the system to liven up areas, such as
the back of the envelope, that have
no other visuals.

PACIFIC COAST FEATHER COMPANY • 1964 FOURTH AVE. S. • BOX 80385 • SEATTLE, WA • 98108 • USA
PHONE: (206)624-1057 • FAX: (206)625-9783

Art Directors/Studio Silvio Silva Junior, Karine Mitsui Kawamura/ Studio Lúmen

Designers/Studio Silvio Silva Junior, Karine Mitsui Kawamura/Studio Lúmen

Client/Service Bastidores/costumes for film and theater

Type Galliard, Futura Condensed

Colors Two, process, and one, match

Printing Offset

Software CorelDRAW, Adobe Streamline

Billable Hours to Complete 20 (senior designer), 16 (junior designer), 12 (trainee)

Concept An illustration of a traditional theatrical mask, combined with the pattern of yellow dots (suggestive of theatrical lights), conveys the client's business—costuming for theater and film.

Special Visual Effects Extra visual touches, such as the clever type treatments on the back of the business card and the envelope, give this system appeal.

Cost $4,641

Art Directors/Studio Sonia Greteman, James Strange/Greteman Group
Designers/Studio Sonia Greteman, James Strange/Greteman Group
Client/Service Anita Fréy/property management
Paper Beckett Concept Meadow
Type Optima
Colors Two, match
Printing Offset
Software Aldus FreeHand
Billable Hours to Complete 24

Concept The combination of a cloud motif with the subtle use of a key symbol suggests the client's business —property management—without being clichéd. This unusual motif, coupled with a strong color treatment, makes this system stand out from the client's competitors.

Special Production Techniques The clouds were screened from dark to light to add space and drama to the system.

Special Visual Effects Unusual visual touches, such as the photos of employees on their business cards and the use of a small key symbol to denote where text should be placed on the letterhead and envelope, are both functional and engaging.

Budget $3,000
Initial Print Run 5,000

Art Directors/Studio Sam Shelton, Jeff Fabian/KINETIK Communications Graphics, Inc.
Designers/Studio Sam Shelton/ KINETIK Communications Graphics, Inc.
Illustrator Sam Shelton
Client/Service Susan Gage Catering/catering
Paper Strathmore Writing
Type Futura Condensed, Garamond

Colors One, match
Printing Offset with embossing

Concept The client wanted an identity that reflected their meticulous presentation and gourmet cuisine; the blind-embossed image, complemented by an understated type treatment, is a clean and subtle signifier of the client's classic good taste.
Initial Print Run 1,500

Art Director/Studio John Sayles/
Sayles Graphic Design
Designer/Studio John Sayles/Sayles
Graphic Design
Illustrator John Sayles
Client/Service Acumen Group/target
marketing consulting firm
Paper James River Graphika!
Parchment White
Type Helvetica (name), Times
(address)
Colors Two, black and match
Printing Offset

Concept The client's name (Acumen
Group) and purpose (target marketing consulting) lend themselves
beautifully to a simple visual: a target, combined with the company's
monogram shaped into an arrow.
Special Production Techniques The
target graphic from the logo was
enlarged and printed in 100 percent
match red for drama on both the
back of the letterhead and the interior
of the envelope. Because the paper is
a writing grade, the target shows
through to the front side, giving the
effect of a screen.
Initial Print Run 1,000

Art Director/Studio Sonia Greteman/ Greteman Group

Designers/Studio Sonia Greteman, Karen Hogan/Greteman Group

Client/Service GreenAcres/health food store

Paper Neenah Classic Laid Peppered Bronze

Type Goudy

Colors Two, match

Printing Offset

Software Aldus FreeHand

Billable Hours to Complete 24

Concept A rustic illustrative approach and an earthy color palette are appropriate for the client's business—health foods.

Special Visual Effects Images from the logo were incorporated into the background of the letterhead and envelope, carrying through the sky and meadow motifs from the logo throughout the system and giving it visual coherence.

Cost $3,000

Initial Print Run 5,000

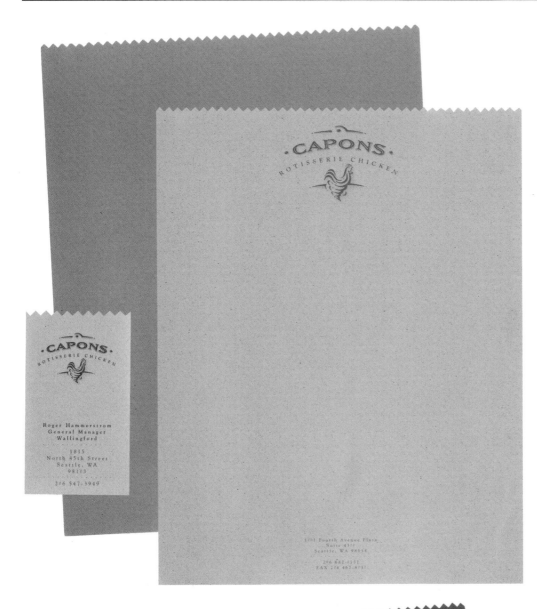

Art Director/Studio Jack Anderson/ Hornall Anderson Design Works
Designers/Studio Jack Anderson, David Bates/Hornall Anderson Design Works
Illustrators David Bates, George Tanagi
Client/Service Capons Rotisserie Chicken/take-out restaurants
Paper Neenah Classic Laid Writing Peppered Bronze
Type Goudy, hand-lettering
Colors Three, match
Printing Offset
Software Aldus FreeHand, QuarkXPress

Concept This system for a chain of take-out chicken restaurants communicates its essence efficiently, with the illustration of the chicken rendered as a spinning tornado conveying the quick nature of the chain. This concept is further communicated by the zigzag edge of the stationery components, which are meant to mimic take-out bags.
Special Visual Effects The use of recycled paper, a sophisticated color scheme and full-bleed colors on the back of the stationery communicate the upscale nature of the chain.

Low
Budget

Working within boundaries to create something that expands them is a challenge all creative people face. It's a challenge shared by many, including poets, musicians and the designers represented in this chapter, who faced down the constraints of small budgets to create work they may never have dreamed up if they had had lots of money to throw at their problems.

If the systems shown in this section have one thing in common (that is, besides their small budgets), it would be the strength of the concepts behind them. As these systems prove, a clever idea can take the viewer's attention away from the cheapest paper stock and the simplest one-color print job.

Making the most of a little, and making it all look easy, is the hallmark of much great art—from poetry to pop music to graphic design.

Art Director/Studio Mark Ford/
Swieter Design
Designer/Studio Mark Ford/Swieter
Design
Illustrator Mark Ford/Swieter Design
Client/Service Dick Patrick Studio/
photography
Paper Champion Benefit
Type Officina
Colors Three, black and match
Printing Offset
Software Adobe Illustrator

Concept Paper stock with a retro
color scheme gives eye-catching
appeal to this simply designed system
for a photographer.
Special Visual Effects Overprinting
type in black on a white-inked background makes the body copy easier to
read on the darker-color paper stock
and adds an extra visual dimension to
the piece.

Dick Patrick Studios 2336 Farrington Street Dallas, Texas 75207
Studio 214/638/8394 Facsimile 214/638/8396 Internet dpstudios@aol.com

Dick Patrick Studios
2336 Farrington Street
Dallas, Texas 75207

Dick Patrick   *photographer*

Dick Patrick Studios
2336 Farrington Street
Dallas, Texas 75207
Studio 214/638/8394
Facsimile 214/638/8396
Internet dpstudios@aol.com

Designer/Studio Eric Kass/Eric Kass Design

Client/Service Admission for One, Inc./custom home theater and audio systems

Paper French Newsprint (letterhead), French Construction (business card), Kraft (envelope)

Type Franklin Gothic, News Gothic

Colors One, black (letterhead, envelope); two, black and match (business card)

Printing Offset and laser

Software Adobe Illustrator

Billable Hours to Complete 12

Concept In this system for a custom home theater company, a logo depicting an amazed customer, coupled with the ticketlike color and design of the business cards, nicely conveys the company's business while playing off its name.

Cost-Cutting Techniques The simplicity of the design allows the letterhead and envelopes to be printed as needed on the client's laser printer.

Cost $310

Initial Print Run 1,000

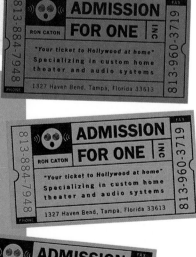

220, Mgr-de-Belmon, Boucherville (Québec) J4B 2K9

Art Directors/Studio George Fok,
Daniel Fortin/Tarzan
Communications Inc.
Designers/Studio George Fok,
Daniel Fortin/Tarzan
Communications Inc.
Client/Service Theâtre Motus/
experimental theater
Paper Domtar Bécasseau
Type Gie (custom-designed), hand-
lettering
Colors One, match
Printing Offset
Software Adobe Photoshop, Adobe
Illustrator, Adobe Streamline

Concept The client's name, which
means "movement" in Latin, called
for this dynamic hand-lettered solution, which simulates the abstract
and energetic form of modern experimental dance and theater.
Cost-Cutting Techniques Using just
one color kept costs down.
Initial Print Run 1,000

Théâtre MOTUS
220, Mgr-de-Belmon, Boucherville (Québec) J4B 2K9
Tél : (514) 655-7291

Art Director/Studio Jesse James
Doquilo/Studio MD
Designer/Studio Jesse James
Doquilo/Studio MD
Client/Service Joan Ross
Blaedel/fine art
Paper Simpson Starwhite Vicksburg
Type Sabon Small Caps
Colors One, match
Printing Offset with embossing and
die cut
Software Aldus FreeHand
Billable Hours to Complete 25

Concept The simple motif of the leaf
in this system for a fine artist suggests the nature of the artist's work,
which is inspired by nature and
organic shapes.
Special Production Techniques The
letterhead uses a sculptured leaf-
shaped emboss die; the business card
is die cut in a leaf shape.
Cost $1,500 (printing and produc-
tion only; design fee traded for fine
art)
Initial Print Run 1,000

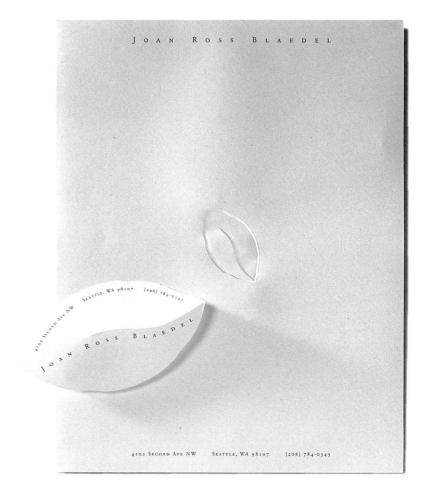

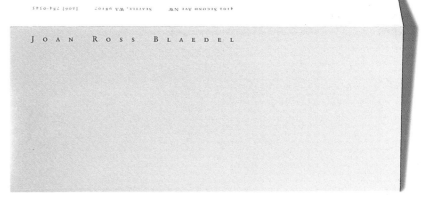

Art Director/Studio Paula Sloane/
Callahan & Co.
Designer/Studio Paula Sloane/
Callahan & Co.
Illustrator Jonathan Carlson
Client/Service Jonathan
Carlson/illustration
Paper French Speckletone Oatmeal
Type City (Light)
Colors Two, black and match
Printing Offset
Software QuarkXPress
Billable Hours to Complete 6

Concept The rich, nostalgic ink and
paper colors all complement the
illustration and help to convey more
about the illustrator's style, which is
evocative of advertising art from the
1930s and 1940s. While the paper
color lends a feeling of antiquity, it
also seems current with today's interest in natural and recycled products.
Cost-Cutting Techniques Limited
ink colors and the use of a low-cost
printer kept costs down
Cost $1,220
Initial Print Run 3,000

Art Directors/Studio Hal Apple,
Karen Walker/Hal Apple Design,
Inc.

Designers/Studio Karen Walker, Hal
Apple/Hal Apple Design, Inc.

Client/Service Hal Apple Design,
Inc./design

Paper French Speckletone

Type Attic, Adobe Garamond,
Orator

Colors One, match

Printing Offset with die cut

Software QuarkXPress

Billable Hours to Complete 30

Concept To communicate the energetic, professional, yet casual nature
of this design firm, the designers
used a combination of rough-hewn
typography and a stencil-like die cut.

Special Production Techniques
Black-and-white photographs of the
text type, complete with cellophane
tape, comprised the camera-ready
artwork.

Cost-Cutting Techniques The same
die was used for all the pieces. Only
one ink color was used.

Cost $2,000

Initial Print Run 2,500

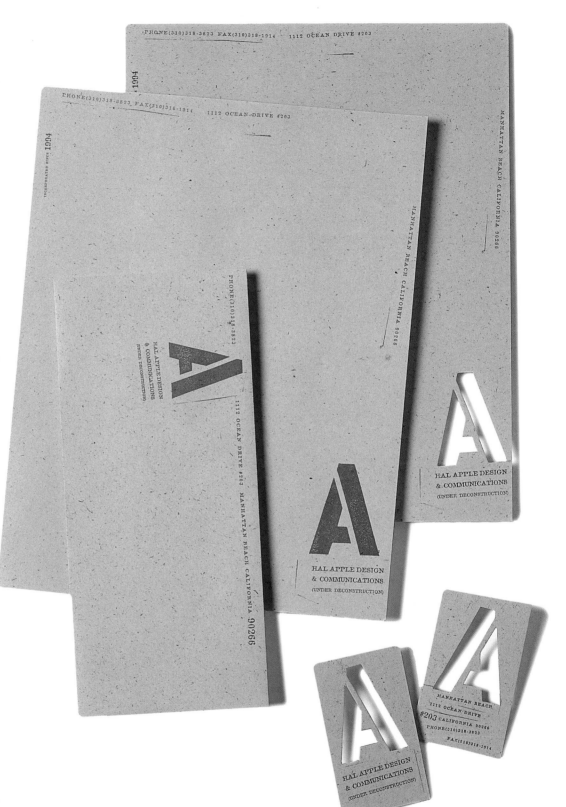

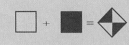

6631 n. glenwood
chicago, il 60626
ph. 312.262.2652   fax 312.262.2653

Art Director/Studio Eric Masi/Masi
Graphica Ltd.
Designer/Studio Eric Masi/Masi
Graphica Ltd.
Illustrator Eric Masi
Client/Service Heather E. Mackinder/
project management
Paper Neenah Classic Crest
Sawgrass (envelope), Tarragon
(letterhead)
Type Party Plain, ITC Kabel
Colors Two, match
Printing Offset
Software QuarkXPress, Adobe
Illustrator
Billable Hours to Complete 15-16

Concept A simple graphic concept
conveys at a glance the client's ability
to solve problems creatively.
Cost-Cutting Techniques The paper
colors used in this system augment
the two ink colors used, while the
pared-down graphics are flexible and
easy to print.
Cost $975
  Initial Print Run 1,200

expect the
unexpected

6631 n. glenwood
chicago, il 60626
ph. 312.262.2652   fax 312.262.2653

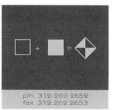

expect the
unexpected

Heather E.
Mackinder

Design
and
Project Management
ph. 312.262.2652
fax 312.262.2653

ph. 312.262.2652
fax 312.262.2653

Art Director/Studio Rodney Davidson/DogStar

Designer/Studio Rodney Davidson/DogStar

Illustrator Rodney Davidson

Client/Service DogStar/design and illustration

Paper Hammermill laser paper (letterhead, business card); Strathmore black art paper (back of business card)

Type Nicolas Cochin, Pritchard, Cappio

Colors One, black, plus multicolor hand-stamping

Printing Laser with multicolor hand-stamping

Software QuarkXPress, Adobe Illustrator, Adobe Photoshop

Billable Hours to Complete 2

Concept This designer came up with a special "tidbits" logo for his pro bono projects. The name was in honor of the "tidbits" a designer usually has to work with on such projects and in honor of a childhood pet of the designer. The use of a dog logo tied in with the name of the firm and with the "pet project" nature of the pro bono work involved.

The overall look is meant to resemble the kind of look the designer would create for one of his pro bono projects.

Cost-Cutting Techniques The "tidbits" logo is hand stamped on the designer's pre-existing stationery as needed.

Cost $.10 per piece

Initial Print Run As needed

Designer/Studio Eric Kass/Eric Kass Design

Client/Service Tracy R. Ball/copy-writing

Paper French Dur-o-tone Newsprint (letterhead), Fox River Confetti (business card), Kraft (envelope)

Type Typewriter

Colors One, black

Printing Rubber-stamping

Software Adobe Illustrator

Billable Hours to Complete 4

Concept Combining a clever logo based on the client's name with simple typewriter type that suggests what she does and color stocks that convey her personality, the designer of this system made the most of this no-budget project.

Cost-Cutting Techniques This system employs paper samples from paper promotions and a rubber stamp (for the client's logo) to cut production costs to a bare minimum.

Cost $60

Initial Print Run As needed

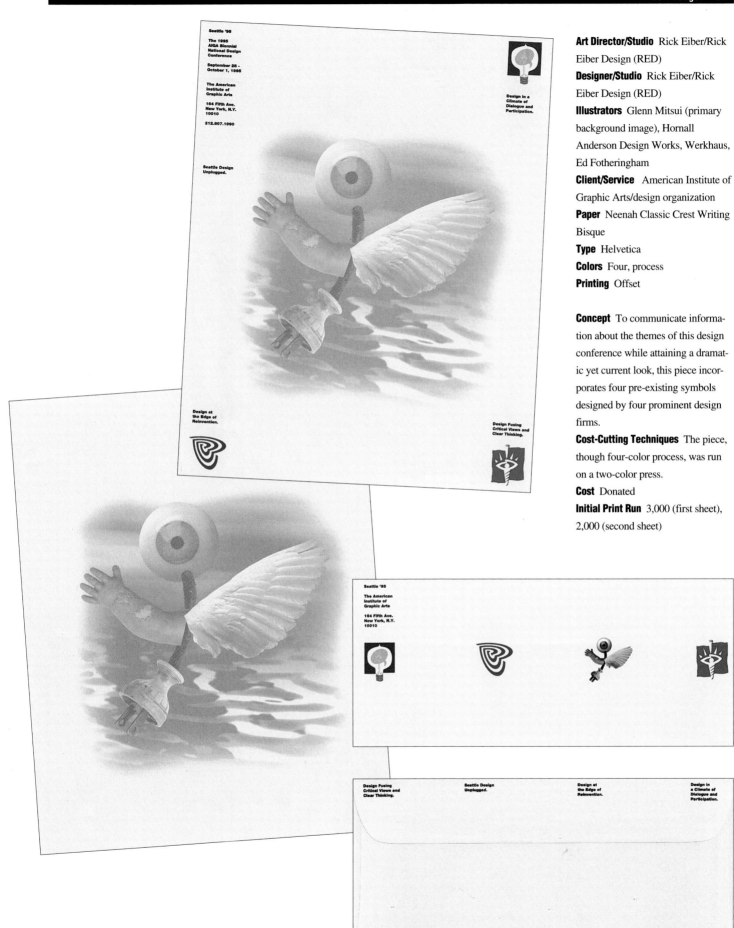

Art Director/Studio Rick Eiber/Rick Eiber Design (RED)

Designer/Studio Rick Eiber/Rick Eiber Design (RED)

Illustrators Glenn Mitsui (primary background image), Hornall Anderson Design Works, Werkhaus, Ed Fotheringham

Client/Service American Institute of Graphic Arts/design organization

Paper Neenah Classic Crest Writing Bisque

Type Helvetica

Colors Four, process

Printing Offset

Concept To communicate information about the themes of this design conference while attaining a dramatic yet current look, this piece incorporates four pre-existing symbols designed by four prominent design firms.

Cost-Cutting Techniques The piece, though four-color process, was run on a two-color press.

Cost Donated

Initial Print Run 3,000 (first sheet), 2,000 (second sheet)

Art Director/Studio Lanny
Sommese/Sommese Design
Designer/Studio Lanny Sommese/
Sommese Design
Client/Service Lanny Sommese/
design, illustration, education and
writing
Paper Scott Index White
Type Futura
Colors One, black
Printing Offset
Software QuarkXPress
Billable Hours to Complete 3

Concept The designer needed three
different business cards because of
the different types of projects he was
involved in, so he came up with this
flexible solution, which can be
detached or folded in a variety of
ways.
Cost-Cutting Techniques The job
was printed in one color on one side
and was delivered flat. Since the
print run was so small, the cards
were trimmed and folded in-house
on an as-needed basis.
Cost Less than $100
Initial Print Run 250

Designer/Studio Michael Calleia/
Industrial Strength Design
Client/Service Industrial Strength
Design/design
Paper French Dur-o-tone Packing
Carton
Type Goudy Sans (display), Seagull
(body, back)
Colors Two over one, match
Printing Letterpress
Software Adobe Illustrator, Adobe
Photoshop
Billable Hours to Complete 2
(design), 10 (printing)

Concept To expand the letterpress
printing side of their business, the
studio designed this card to demonstrate the tactile quality of their printing and to demonstrate that clean
impressions and tight traps were
possible with letterpress. Even more
importantly, it communicates the
diversity of the work the studio is
involved in.
Cost $100
Initial Print Run 1,000

Donna Schumacher
architect

X:architecture/Art

27 South Park | San Francisco, CA 94107 | Phone/Fax 415.543.5720

Art Director/Studio Bill Reuter/
Reuter Design
Designers/Studio Bill Reuter,
Hannele Riihiniemi/Reuter Design
Client/Service X:architecture/Art/
architecture
Paper Hopper Proterra Natural
Cover and Text
Type Univers, Clarendon
Colors Two, black and match
Printing Offset
Software Adobe Illustrator,
QuarkXPress
Billable Hours to Complete 15

Concept The client's company name
is meant to symbolize her dual inter-
ests in art and architecture. This dual-
ity is likewise expressed in the logo,
where a serif typeface is used for one
"a" and a sans serif is used for the
other, and serif and sans serif faces
are combined in the letter "x". The
structural placement of both type and
line suggests the client's occupation.
Cost $1,500
Initial Print Run 1,000

Donna Schumacher
architect

X:architecture/Art
27 South Park
San Francisco, CA 94107
Phone/Fax 415.543.5720

Donna Schumacher
architect

X:architecture/Art
27 South Park
San Francisco, CA 94107
Phone/Fax 415.543.5720

Lovely Walloona

CONFLICT AT THE HEMINGWAYS

THE HEMINGWAY
FOUNDATION
OF OAK PARK
AND THE FRIENDS
OF THE PLAY

600 N. KENILWORTH
OAK PARK, IL 60302

Lovely Walloona

CONFLICT AT THE HEMINGWAYS

A PLAY WRITTEN BY
MORRIS BUSKE

PRESENTED IN
COOPERATION WITH
THE HEMINGWAY
FOUNDATION OF
OAK PARK AND
THE FRIENDS OF
THE PLAY

600 N. KENILWORTH
OAK PARK, IL 60302
708.848.0356

FRIENDS OF THE PLAY
Wallis Austin
Barbara Ballinger
Wes Boyer
Mercita DeMuynck
Doug Deuchler
Gloria Garafalo
Carol Gibson
Elsie Jacobsen
Waring Jones
Pete Mavrelis
Paula Nelson
Donald Offermann
John Philbin
Bobbie Raymond
Art Replogle
Scott Schwar

Art Director/Studio Nicholas Sinadinos/Nicholas Associates
Designers/Studio Nicholas Sinadinos, Scott Hardy/Nicholas Associates
Illustrator Scott Hardy
Photographer Unknown
Client/Service The Ernest Hemingway Foundation/play
Paper Simpson EverGreen Aspen
Type Yorkshire (headline), Scala (text)
Colors Two, match
Printing Offset
Software Adobe Photoshop, Aldus FreeHand
Billable Hours to Complete 16

Concept For this stationery for a play about a rift between Ernest Hemingway and his mother, the designer combined torn photographs of the two. The imperfect image quality that resulted from the poor originals at hand suggests a dark \ mood that contrasts graphically with the decorative script used for the title of the play.
Cost-Cutting Techniques Using found images, inexpensive paper stock and only two colors helped keep costs down.
Cost $1,000
Initial Print Run 2,500

Art Director/Studio Dan Flynn/
Vaughn/Wedeen Creative
Designer/Studio Dan Flynn/
Vaughn/Wedeen Creative
Illustrator Dan Flynn
Client/Service Horizon Healthcare,
Inc./rehabilitation center
Paper Simpson Starwhite Vicksburg
Archiva Writing
Type Bodoni
Colors Two, match
Printing Offset
Software QuarkXPress

Concept A gentle and relaxed illustration style and color scheme give
this system for a rehabilitation center
a restful look.
Cost-Cutting Techniques Using only
two colors on each piece helped keep
costs down.
Initial Print Run 5,000

C O M M U N I T Y
R E H A B I L I T A T I O N
C E N T E R S ,   I N C .

913 Warren-Youngstown Road, Suite C • Niles, Ohio 44556 • 216·544·0300 • 800·846·2695 • FAX 216·544·0511

6001 Indian School Road NE. • Albuquerque, New Mexico 87110

C O M M U N I T Y
R E H A B I L I T A T I O N
C E N T E R S ,   I N C .

C O M M U N I T Y
R E H A B I L I T A T I O N
C E N T E R S ,   I N C .

Beth Irtz
Director of
Rehabilitation Services

Cherry Creek Place I
3131 S. Vaughn Way, Suite 405
Aurora, Colorado 80014
303·369·9685
FAX 303·369·0609

Art Director/Studio Lance Anderson/
Lance Anderson Design
Designer/Studio Lance Anderson/
Lance Anderson Design
Client/Service International
Marketing and Media/marketing and
media
Paper Starwhite Vicksburg Tiara
White Smooth Finish (letterhead,
envelope); Strathmore Writing Cover
Bristol (business card)
Type Univers, Bernhard
Colors Two, black and match
Printing Offset
Printer Logos Graphics, San
Francisco
Software QuarkXPress, Adobe
Illustrator
Billable Hours to Complete 30

Concept A simple typographic
interpretation of the client's initials,
coupled with a pared-down but strik-
ing color scheme, is enough to give
this system for a marketing and
media firm a prestigious look.
Cost $2,000
Initial Print Run 2,500

International Marketing and Media

3 Hart Lane, Mill Valley, California 94941
T - 415 380 8918 F - 415 380 9601 CompuServe - 74041.3434

International Marketing and Media

3 Hart Lane, Mill Valley, California 94941

International Marketing and Media

Edie Ohamoto - President
3 Hart Lane
Mill Valley
California 94941
T - 415 380 8918
F - 415 380 9601
CompuServe - 74041.3434

Designer/Studio Michael Calleia/
Industrial Strength Design
Illustrator Michael Calleia
Client/Service Limbo/cafe
Paper Strathmore Writing White
Card
Type Avant Garde Gothic
Colors Two, black and match
Printing Offset
Software Adobe Illustrator, Adobe
Photoshop
Billable Hours to Complete 1.5

Concept The interactive component
of this business card cleverly alludes
to the client's name, while the faux
coffee ring on the back of the card
that completes the name when the
card is held by the string on either
side refers to the client's business—a
cafe.
Special Production Techniques The
coffee stain was scanned from a real
coffee stain created for the project.
Cost-Cutting Techniques The design
studio bought the die itself and did
the die cutting on a letterpress, keeping costs low.
Cost $480
Initial Print Run 1,000

Art Director/Studio Brian Miller/
Love Packaging Group
Designer/Studio Brian Miller/Love
Packaging Group
Illustrator Brian Miller
Client/Service Ruth and Charles
Miller/distributors of gourmet
coffees
Paper Multiple stocks from other
jobs (primarily Fox River Circa
Ivory and Champion Benefit Natural
Straw)
Type Bank Gothic (address, name);
Atlas (tag line); hand-modified
Matrix Script and Davison
Americana (logo)

Colors One, match
Printing Offset
Software Aldus FreeHand, Adobe
Photoshop
Billable Hours to Complete 8

Concept An eye-catching, oversized
format and a coffee-and-cream color
motif convey the client's business
uniquely and succinctly.

Cost-Cutting Techniques The design
was conceived as an inexpensive
one-color job, and an inexpensive
commercial printer printed the job for
one-third of what bigger printing
houses had quoted. Leftover paper
stock from other jobs was used, and
the client cut the cards himself.
Cost $540
Initial Print Run 500

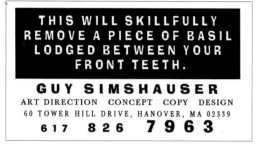

Art Director/Studio Guy Simshauser/ Simshauser Creative

Designer/Studio Guy Simshauser/ Simshauser Creative

Client/Service Simshauser Creative/freelance creative services

Paper Hopper Sunray Cover

Type Blox, Baskerville MT

Colors One, black

Printing Laser

Software QuarkXPress, Adobe Illustrator

Billable Hours to Complete 3

Concept The simplicity of this design for a freelance creative service allows the humorous concept to sell this designer's ability to take a creative risk.

Cost-Cutting Techniques The designer created a template in QuarkXPress, printed the front of the business card on his laser printer, then flipped the paper and printed the other side in register. The designer then hand-trimmed the card.

Cost $175

Initial Print Run 100

Designer/Studio David Lomeli/ Man?Bot! Design

Client/Service Man?Bot! Design/ graphic design

Paper Simpson Quest

Type Din Engschrift, Din Neuzeit Grotesk Condensed Bold

Colors Two, match

Printing Offset

Software Adobe Illustrator

Concept This folded business card graphically explains the origins of the design firm's name.

Cost–Cutting Techniques Since this piece was tagged onto another print job, it cost the designer nothing.

Cost $0

Initial Print Run 1,000

Art Director Ralph Watson

Designer/Studio Rodney Davidson/ DogStar

Illustrator Rodney Davidson

Client/Service Jimmie Hale Mission/ mission for the homeless

Paper Neenah Environment Desert Storm

Type Trixie, Senator

Colors One, black

Printing Offset

Software QuarkXPress, Aldus FreeHand

Billable Hours to Complete 35

Concept This system was designed to mark the fiftieth anniversary of a homeless shelter. The logo suggests the two things the mission provides: food and shelter. The rough type treatment and paper stock and simple one-color printing are appropriately sober choices for this nonprofit mission.

Cost-Cutting Techniques Originally the designer wanted to have the black bar bleed off the bottom of the letterhead, but realizing how costly it would be, he placed the bar at the bottom of the page with a little white space around it, achieving a similar effect for less cost.

Cost $90 (printing expenses only; design, illustration and paper donated)

Initial Print Run 1,000 (envelope), 1,500 (letterhead), 500 (business card)

Art Director/Studio Joel Blum/Pace Design Group

Designer/Studio Joel Blum/Pace Design Group

Photo-Illustrator Joel Blum

Photographer Found

Client/Service Pace Design Group/graphic design for marketing communications

Paper Neenah Classic Crest Writing; Avon Brilliant White (letterhead, envelope); Potlatch Vintage Velvet Cover (business card)

Type Univers Black Light Condensed and Light Condensed Italic, vintage typewriter

Colors Four over four, process (business card); two, match (all other pieces)

Printing Offset

Software QuarkXPress, Adobe Photoshop

Billable Hours to Complete 30

Concept The designer of this system took advantage of the opportunity to design for a less traditional client—his own firm—by coming up with this tongue-in-cheek system.

Cost-Cutting Techniques The portraits are from a 1960s yearbook salvaged from the city dump (the blackout bars had a practical purpose: to help prevent subjects from recognizing themselves). On the business cards, the firm shared a press sheet with another design firm, enabling the client to afford four over four process color.

Cost $2,392.50 (production and printing only)

Initial Print Run 500 (presentation folder), 1,500 (all other pieces)

Art Director/Studio Rick Sealock/ Maverick Art Tribe

Designer/Studio Rick Sealock/ Maverick Art Tribe

Illustrator Rick Sealock

Client/Service Rick Sealock/illustration

Paper Cross Pointe Bright Canary (letterhead), MacTac Crack and Peel (sticker, business card)

Type Hand-lettering, found

Colors Three, black and match

Printing Offset

Billable Hours to Complete 10

Concept Inspired by the comic book ads of his youth, this illustrator came up with a system that amply displays his over-the-top approach to illustration. Bright colors and ransom-note-style typography complete the no-holds-barred look the illustrator was going for.

Special Production Techniques Printing much of the system on stickers allowed the illustrator flexibility in its use.

Cost $537.17

Initial Print Run 500 (letterhead), 250 (sticker)

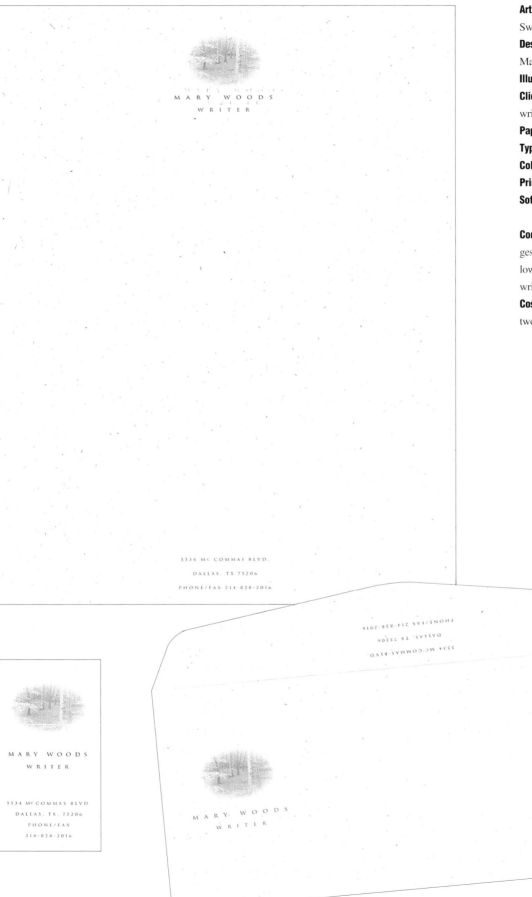

Art Director/Studio John Swieter/
Swieter Design
Designers/Studio John Swieter,
Mark Ford/Swieter Design
Illustrator John Swieter
Client/Service Mary Woods/copy-
writing
Paper Cross Pointe Genesis Birch
Type Trajan
Colors Two, match
Printing Offset
Software Adobe Illustrator

Concept Using an illustration suggestive of the client's name was a
low-key solution for this system for a
writer.
Cost-Cutting Techniques Using only
two colors cut costs.

Art Director/Studio Barbara Bruch/
Barbara Bruch Design
Designer/Studio Barbara Bruch/
Barbara Bruch Design
Client/Service Barbara Bruch
Design/graphic design
Paper Crane Crest
Colors Two, match
Printing Offset
Software QuarkXPress

Concept Floral illustrations and two
shades of green were a fitting solution for this system for a graphic
designer who may expand her business to include landscape design.
Coordinating notecards use flower-
related quotations to continue the
theme.
Cost-Cutting Techniques For illustrations, the designer used old botan-
ical illustrations scanned in from a
book of public domain artwork.
Cost Donated
Initial Print Run 500

PHOTO DISTRICT

NEIGHBORHOOD

ASSOCIATION

2412 Converse Street, Dallas, TX 75207, Ph 214.631.7606, Fax 214.951.0424

Art Director/Studio Bryan L. Peterson/Peterson & Co.
Designer/Studio Bryan L. Peterson/ Peterson & Co.
Client/Service Robb Debenport/ photography
Paper Generic bond
Type Bell Gothic Bold
Colors One, black
Printing Letterpress
Software QuarkXPress, Adobe Illustrator
Billable Hours to Complete 5

Concept To symbolize a united effort for awareness and cooperation among photographers in the face of an elevated crime rate in the Dallas Photo District, the logo for this system neatly combines the ideas of photography and awareness.
Cost-Cutting Techniques A simple one-color letterpress job on bond paper kept costs down.
Initial Print Run 500

PHOTO DISTRICT

NEIGHBORHOOD

ASSOCIATION

2412 Converse Street, Dallas, TX 75207, Ph 214.631.7606, Fax 214.951.0424

Art Director/Studio Jamie Sheehan/
Sheehan Design
Designer/Studio Jamie Sheehan/
Sheehan Design
Illustrator Jamie Sheehan
Client/Service Sheehan Design/
graphic design
Paper Simpson Starwhite
Vicksburg Smooth Tiara White
Type Retro Bold ("d'sign"), Orator
(copy)
Colors Two, black and match
Printing Offset
Software QuarkXPress

Concept This designer wanted to
come up with a system that would
get noticed in a stack of mail; her use
of an all-over, fluorescent graphic on
the envelope ensures that her correspondence will stand out. Variations
on this graphic are picked up on all
the other components; the graphic
pattern on the letterhead is meant to
be used as the left-hand margin for
all the designer's laser-printed correspondence.
Special Production Techniques The
pattern used throughout was hand-
drawn on the mechanicals and printed in fluorescent ink that was mixed
to match the designer's highlighter
pen.
Special Visual Effects Because of
the fluorescent ink on the back, a
halo effect is achieved around the
card when it's placed on a light-
colored surface.
Cost $1,156.50 (printing)
Initial Print Run 1,000

Designer Paula Brinkman
Illustrator Paula Brinkman
Client/Service Paula Brinkman/
illustration and design
Paper Card stock
Type Hand-lettering
Colors One, black
Printing Thermography

Concept This illustrator's business
card uses a whimsical self-portrait to
convey the personality of her work.
Cost-Cutting Techniques Printing all
the cards in black and white saved
money and allowed the illustrator to
express her creativity through hand
coloring or rubber stamping a variety
of colors and patterns on individual
cards.
Cost $149.95
Initial Print Run 1,000 of each

Art Director/Studio Gunnar Swanson/
Gunnar Swanson Design Office

Designer/Studio Gunnar Swanson/
Gunnar Swanson Design Office

Client/Service Gunnar Swanson
Design Office/graphic design

Paper Curtis Parchkin Riblaid (letterhead), Gamalope (envelope),
Gilclear (business card)

Type Hadriano

Colors Two plus laser (letterhead),
one plus laser (envelope), two over
two, match (business card)

Printing Offset and laser

Software Adobe Illustrator,
Microsoft Word

Billable Hours to Complete 10-15

Concept This design firm is current-
ly in temporary quarters and needed
a limited but unknown quantity of
letterhead to tide it over until perma-
nent quarters were found. By designing a solution that allowed the
address information to be laser-printed as needed, this studio came up
with a flexible system that would
work for it until (and maybe even
after) it moved.

Cost-Cutting Techniques The use of
vellum gives this low-budget system
a high-end look.

Cost $500

Initial Print Run 500

Type

It's a given that type is a cornerstone of great design, but nowhere is type more crucial than with letterhead and business cards. After all, if you're corresponding with people, you want them to know how to reach you, and if you're handing others your business card, you want them to remember your name. When designing letterhead and business cards, even for the trendiest of clients, readability is key.

But, as the 30 solutions in this chapter prove, type can be readable without being boring. Simply laying out a traditional type-face in an unconventional way—as Matsumoto Incorporated did for Michael Maharam—can give a system a creative twist without impeding communication. Or combining straightforward type with type that takes the place of a graphic—as Sackett Design Associates did for Bybee Studios— can make a system typographically clear but still up-to-the-minute. Let these myriad solutions to the same old dilemma inspire you to use type to its best advantage.

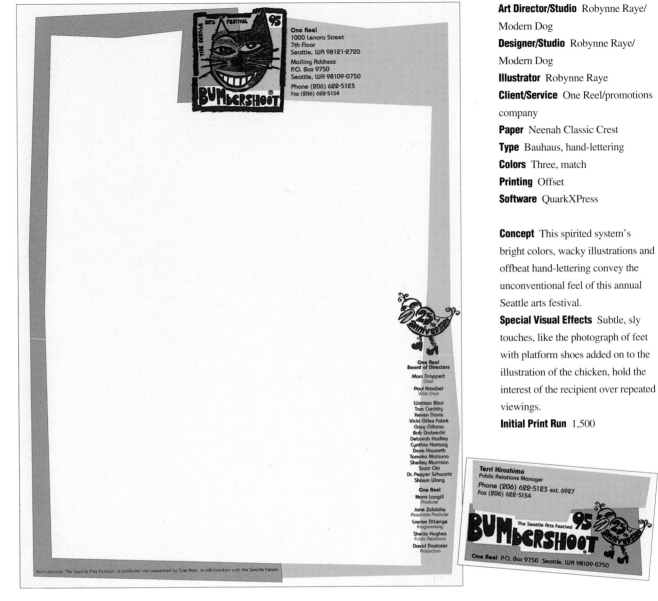

Art Director/Studio Robynne Raye/
Modern Dog
Designer/Studio Robynne Raye/
Modern Dog
Illustrator Robynne Raye
Client/Service One Reel/promotions
company
Paper Neenah Classic Crest
Type Bauhaus, hand-lettering
Colors Three, match
Printing Offset
Software QuarkXPress

Concept This spirited system's
bright colors, wacky illustrations and
offbeat hand-lettering convey the
unconventional feel of this annual
Seattle arts festival.
Special Visual Effects Subtle, sly
touches, like the photograph of feet
with platform shoes added on to the
illustration of the chicken, hold the
interest of the recipient over repeated
viewings.
Initial Print Run 1,500

Art Directors/Studio Jeff Fabian,
Sam Shelton/KINETIK
Communications Graphics, Inc.
Designers/Studio Jeff Fabian, Amy
Gustinere, Mimi Massé/KINETIK
Communications Graphics, Inc.
Client/Service KINETIK
Communications Graphics, Inc./
graphic design
Paper Champion Benefit
Type Meta Plus Book Caps
Colors Two, match
Printing Offset
Software QuarkXPress, Aldus
FreeHand, Adobe Photoshop

Concept The designers used lines,
placement and a white-inked "spine"
as a visual interpretation of the energy and motion associated with the
word "kinetic." The use of unusual
type placement in conjunction with
the lines adds to the interest of the
letterhead.
Special Visual Effects Using a wide
variety of darker paper stocks and
overprinting them with white ink is
an unexpected visual touch.
Initial Print Run 3,000

Le Château des Fêtes

386, RUE LE MOYNE, MONTRÉAL, QUÉBEC H2Y 1Y3
TÉLÉPHONE: (514) 287-0810 TÉLÉCOPIEUR: (514) 287-1247

Art Directors/Studio Daniel Fortin, George Fok/Tarzan Communications Inc.
Designers/Studio George Fok, Daniel Fortin/Tarzan Communications Inc.
Client/Service Les Animeries/drama for children
Paper Strathmore Element
Type Letraset Charlotte
Colors Two, match
Printing Offset
Software Adobe Photoshop, Adobe Illustrator, Adobe Streamline

Concept This charming system for a dramatic troupe for children uses a childlike typeface and illustration style to convey the client's business.
Cost-Cutting Techniques A patterned paper was used to give the effect of a three-color system for the cost of two colors.
Initial Print Run 1,000

Le Château des Fêtes

SUZANNE MORENCY
Directrice générale

386, RUE LE MOYNE, MONTRÉAL, QUÉBEC H2Y 1Y3
TÉLÉPHONE: (514) 654-7669 TÉLÉCOPIEUR: (514) 654-1544

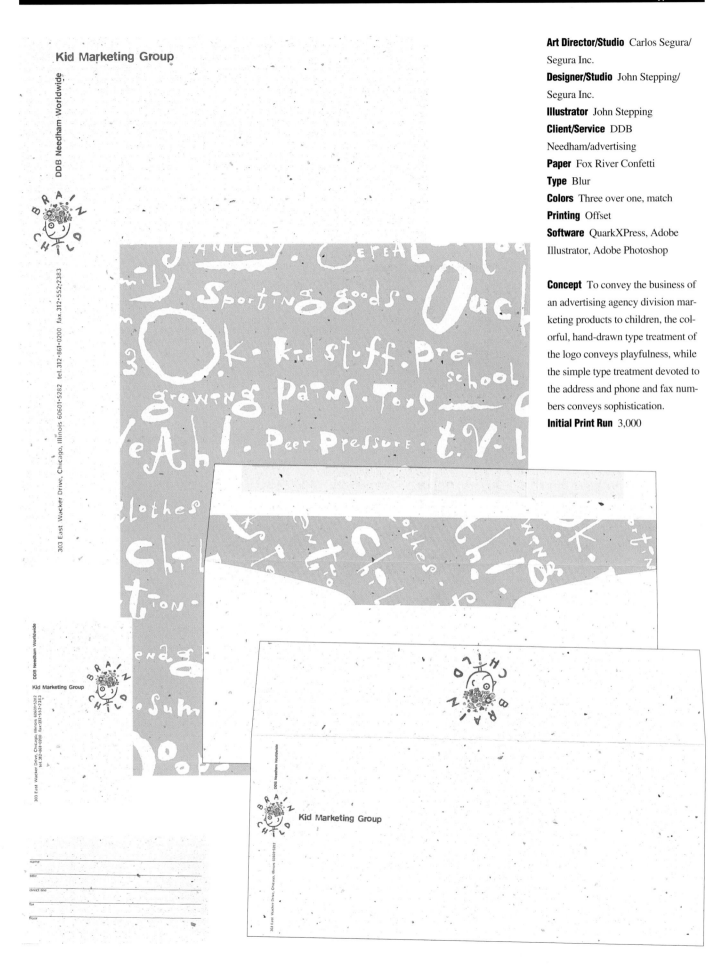

Art Director/Studio Carlos Segura/
Segura Inc.
Designer/Studio John Stepping/
Segura Inc.
Illustrator John Stepping
Client/Service DDB
Needham/advertising
Paper Fox River Confetti
Type Blur
Colors Three over one, match
Printing Offset
Software QuarkXPress, Adobe
Illustrator, Adobe Photoshop

Concept To convey the business of
an advertising agency division marketing products to children, the colorful, hand-drawn type treatment of
the logo conveys playfulness, while
the simple type treatment devoted to
the address and phone and fax numbers conveys sophistication.
Initial Print Run 3,000

Bybee Studios 1811 Folsom Street San Francisco, California 94103-4223

ShaUnBybee

Telephone S.F. 415.863.6346 L.A. 213.463.6288 Facsimile 415.255.1687

Art Director/Studio Mark Sackett/
Sackett Design Associates
Designers/Studio Mark Sackett,
Wayne Sakamoto, James
Sakamoto/Sackett Design Associates
Illustrators Wayne Sakamoto, James
Sakamoto
Client/Service Bybee Studios/
photography
Paper Simpson Starwhite Vicksburg
Type Bauer Bodoni
Colors Two, black and match
Printing Offset
Software Adobe Illustrator

Concept This dynamic all-type treatment is an unusual one for a photographer, but, owing to its flexibility
and its sophistication, it works.
Cost $10,500
Initial Print Run 3,000 (letterhead,
envelope); 1,000 (business card);
7,000 (label)

1811 Folsom Street San Francisco, California 94103-4223 bybeeStudios Tel. S.F. 415.863.6346 L.A. 213.463.6288 Fax 415.255.1687

1811 Folsom Street bybeeStudios San Francisco, CA 94103

Art Director/Studio Vittorio Costarella/Modern Dog
Designer/Studio Vittorio Costarella/ Modern Dog
Client/Service Experience Music Project/Northwest music museum
Paper Simpson Starwhite Vicksburg
Type Avant Garde
Colors Two, match
Printing Offset
Software Adobe Illustrator, QuarkXPress

Concept For the initial phase of the development of a Northwest music museum, the designer came up with this simple letterhead with a retro feel (including its use of Avant Garde, a classic "modern" typeface from the past). The use of a 1960s color scheme was inspired by the emphasis on Jimi Hendrix in the museum.
Cost-Cutting Techniques All pieces were only two colors.
Initial Print Run 2,000

Art Director/Studio Jon Dilley/Jon Dilley Applied Arts
Designer/Studio Jon Dilley/Jon Dilley Applied Arts
Client/Service Allison Leach/photography
Paper French Brown Kraft Offwhite
Type Bailey, Eagle Book
Colors Two, black and match
Printing Offset
Software Adobe Photoshop, Adobe Illustrator, QuarkXPress
Billable Hours to Complete 30

Concept The client liked the retro feel of the designer's previous work and so commissioned him to design an identity for her with a similar look.
Cost-Cutting Techniques The designer used public domain photographs of photographic equipment to save money and to achieve an authentic feel. Using black plus a different match color for each piece, as well as using a variety of paper colors, gives the system extra color at no extra cost.
Cost $2,500
Initial Print Run 2,000

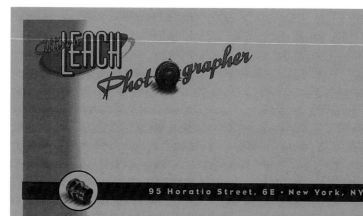

Art Director/Studio John Sayles/
Sayles Graphic Design
Designer/Studio John Sayles/Sayles
Graphic Design
Illustrator John Sayles
Client/Service Timbuktuu Coffee
Bar/coffee bar
Paper Cross Pointe Genesis Tallow
(letterhead), Tortoise (envelope),
Copper (business card)
Type Hand-lettering
Colors Two, match
Printing Offset

Concept This system uses earth colors and a rough-hewn style to play
off the name of the client and uses
coffee beans, cups and spoons to
play off the client's business.
Special Visual Effects The hand-
rendered typeface includes letters
shaped from spoons and coffee cups.
Icon graphics in the program are coffee pots and steaming mugs held over
a fire. Tribal borders maintain the
theme while adding visual interest.
Cost-Cutting Techniques Only two
colors of ink were used, keeping
costs down but providing consistency between pieces. Screens and different colors of paper add visual
interest.
Initial Print Run 2,500

Art Director/Studio John Ball/Mires Design, Inc.

Designers/Studio John Ball, Kathy Carpentier-Moore/Mires Design, Inc.

Photographer Stock

Client/Service Nextec Applications, Inc./fabric-protection technology

Paper Simpson Protocol

Type Goudy Sans, Frutiger

Colors Four, process

Printing Offset with embossing

Software QuarkXPress, Adobe Illustrator

Concept This start-up client, a company that develops technology for making fabrics withstand elements, wanted a fresh and flexible look. This solution, which incorporates photographs of these natural elements into a format akin to a swatch of fabric that has been cut by pinking shears, suggests the client's business. It still remains flexible enough to allow for the use of different photographs in the same format, should the client's business evolve or expand.

Special Production Techniques The combination of four-color process with a registered emboss gives the logo a three-dimensional feel.

Initial Print Run 5,000 (letterhead, envelope); 500 each name (business card)

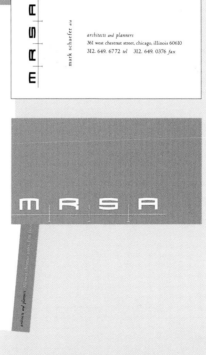

Art Director/Studio Carlos Segura/ Segura Inc.

Designers/Studio Carlos Segura, Jon Stepping/Segura Inc.

Client/Service MRSA Architects/ architecture

Paper Mohawk Ultrafelt

Type Mata, Centaur

Colors Two, black and match

Printing Offset

Software QuarkXPress, Adobe Illustrator

Concept In this system for an architectural firm, a clean type treatment and a sophisticated color scheme put the ridged texture of the paper stock at center stage.

Special Visual Effects The small rules that intersect the rule underlining the logo are so subtly suggestive of nails that the effect is elegant rather than trite.

Initial Print Run 10,000

Microsoft Corporation
One Microsoft Way
Redmond, WA 98052-6399
Tel 206 936 1437
Fax 206 936 7329
Telex 160520 Microsoft BVUE
Internet: annette@microsoft.com

me!

Annette Elsbree
Software Test Engineer
Kids - HPU

-my #

where I ← work

(**Microsoft®**
kids & games unit)

Art Director/Studio Pat Hansen/
Hansen Design Company
Designer/Studio Pat Hansen/Hansen
Design Company
Client/Service Microsoft Kids &
Games Unit/children's software
Paper Karma White Cover
Type Hand-lettering on existing
corporate card
Colors Four, match
Printing Offset
Software Aldus FreeHand
Billable Hours to Complete 18.5

Concept The client requested a
design that would make their current
business cards more fun. By per-
forming "guerilla design" on the
existing card, this solution conveyed
the "kid" aspect of the division while
still retaining the required corporate
look.
Special Production Techniques The
existing corporate colors and identity
signature were overprinted with
bright kidlike match colors.
Cost $1,000 (design and production
only)
Initial Print Run 500 each of 60
names

Art Director/Studio George Fok,
Daniel Fortin/Tarzan
Communications Inc.
Designers/Studio George Fok,
Daniel Fortin/Tarzan
Communications Inc.
Client/Service Nitro-Édition
Digitale/multimedia programming,
digital video editing and data storage
Paper Neenah UV Ultra II
Type Officina ITC
Colors Two, black and match
Printing Offset
Software Adobe Illustrator, Adobe
Photoshop

Concept This business card's fiery
color scheme and dynamic type
treatment provide a fitting visual
interpretation of the name of the
client, who specializes in multimedia
programming, digital video editing
and data storage.
Special Production Techniques A
special mix of metallic orange ink,
printed on a thick vellum, gives this
card a burnished look.
Special Visual Effects A subtle
series of numerals suggestive of
computer processing is ghosted in
the background, giving the card its
unusual textured look.
Initial Print Run 1,000

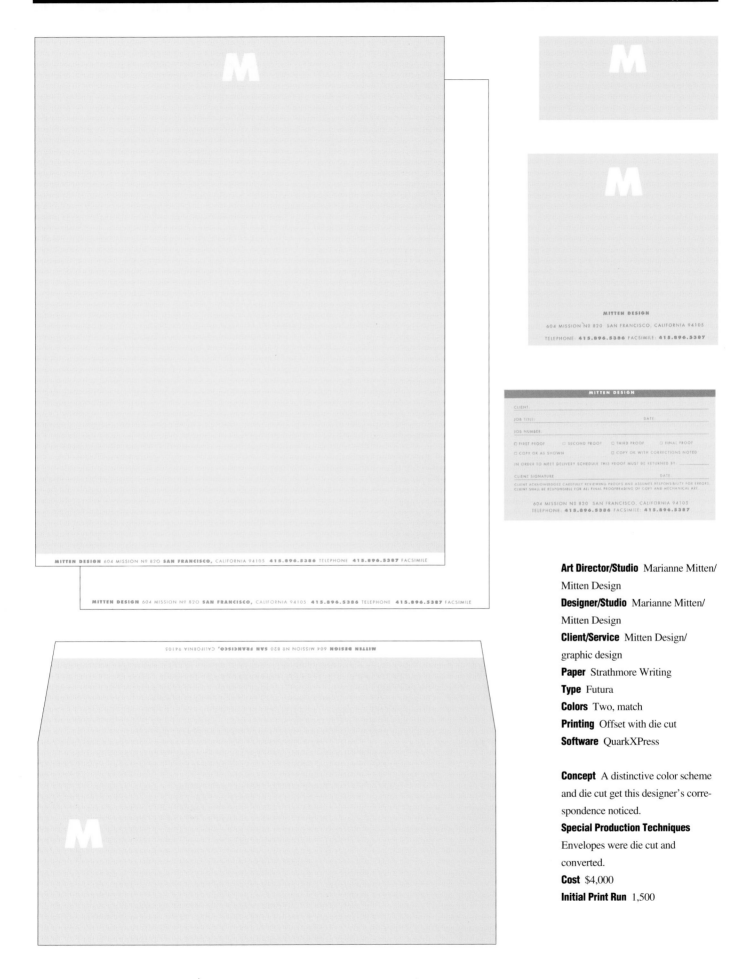

Art Director/Studio Marianne Mitten/
Mitten Design
Designer/Studio Marianne Mitten/
Mitten Design
Client/Service Mitten Design/
graphic design
Paper Strathmore Writing
Type Futura
Colors Two, match
Printing Offset with die cut
Software QuarkXPress

Concept A distinctive color scheme
and die cut get this designer's corre-
spondence noticed.
Special Production Techniques
Envelopes were die cut and
converted.
Cost $4,000
Initial Print Run 1,500

E-Mail: info@goodnet.com
404 South Mill, Ste.C201
Tempe, Arizona 85281
Fax: 602.303.0550
Tel: 602.303.9500

GoodNet

E-Mail: info@goodnet.com
404 South Mill, Ste.C201
Tempe, Arizona 85281

GoodNet

Studio After Hours Creative
Client/Service GoodNet/Internet
service provider
Paper Neenah Classic Crest Avon
Brilliant White
Type OCRB Regular
Colors Two, match
Printing Offset
Software QuarkXPress, Adobe
Illustrator, Adobe Photoshop
Billable Hours to Complete 80

Concept The incorporation of the @ symbol, which is used in all Internet addresses, into the logo for GoodNet makes an immediate link between the company's name and the service it provides—access to the Internet. An up-to-the-minute color scheme communicates the youthfulness of the company, as well as helping the company's mail stand out in a stack.

Special Visual Effects On the back of the letterhead and business card, a collage of photographs printed in vibrant colors suggests the wealth of information accessible on the Internet.
Cost $1,400 (printing only; design fee paid out in equity stake in company)
Initial Print Run 2,000

David W. Brady
dbrady@goodnet.com
404 South Mill, Ste.C201
Tempe, Arizona 85281
Fax: 602.303.0550
Tel: 602.303.9500 #223

GoodNet

Art Director/Studio Stefan
Sagmeister/Sagmeister Inc.
Designer/Studio Stefan Sagmeister/
Sagmeister Inc.
Illustrator Miau Moi
Photographer Tom Schierlitz
Client/Service DHA [USA]/comput-
er and new media consultation

Paper Strathmore Writing
Type Hand-lettering, Courier
Colors One, black
Printing Offset
Software QuarkXPress, Adobe
Illustrator, Adobe Photoshop

Concept This elegant solution for a
computer and new media consulting
firm strikingly conveys the interac-
tion between people and computers.
Cost-Cutting Techniques The use of
photographed type saved money on
typesetting costs.

Special Visual Effects Photographs
were specifically designed to relate to
the piece on which they were used
(with a photograph of a hand used on
the business card, a photograph of a
package used on the label, etc.).

COMMUNICATION
STRATEGIES
5830 N. 12th Place
Suite 5
Phoenix, AZ 85014

Curtis Steinhoff

COMMUNICATION
STRATEGIES
5830 N. 12th Place
Suite 5
Phoenix, AZ 85014
602 650-1566

Copy me on that

We need a committee

Talk to my secretary

How about next week

I love my job

Follow the rules

My computer crashed

It must be the software

My spel check missed it

Think for a change

It hasn't arrived

What was your name

You look familiar

Studio After Hours Creative

Client/Service Communication
Strategies/marketing consultation

Paper Strathmore White

Type Helvetica Bold, Helvetica
Condensed

Colors Two, match

Printing Offset

Software QuarkXPress

Billable Hours to Complete 20

Concept To convey the client's
mission—better business communication—the designer of this system
used a string of common business
clichés, all printed in black, inter-
rupted by only one phrase that's
printed in red: "Think for a change."

Cost-Cutting Techniques The simplicity of the all-type solution, printed with only two colors, saved
money.

Cost $2,500

Initial Print Run 1,000

How long has it been

What a good idea

Just run with it

Let's do lunch

Check's in the mail

Send me a resume

I'll get right on it

I was just about to call

My boss is really nice

I was just leaving

Can we reschedule

Traffic was really bad

I never watch TV

I know a great place

I'm a great driver

Copy me on that

We need a committee

Talk to my secretary

How about next week

I love my job

Follow the rules

My computer crashed

It must be the software

My spel check missed it

I double checked it

It hasn't arrived

What was your name

You look familiar

I hate office politics

Of course we met

Nice tie

Have you lost weight

I workout during lunch

Sorry I'm late

I think it's stress

Think for a change

I know what you mean

Where's my raise

You want it when

COMMUNICATION
STRATEGIES
5830 N. 12th Place
Suite 5
Phoenix, AZ 85014
602 650-1566

Art Director/Studio Petrula
Vrontikis/Vrontikis Design Office
Designer/Studio Petrula Vrontikis/
Vrontikis Design Office
Client/Service Aileen Farnan
Antonier/copywriting
Paper Protocol bond
Type Helvetica
Colors Two, match
Printing Offset lithography
Software QuarkXPress, Adobe
Photoshop
Billable Hours to Complete 20

Concept The client, a copywriter,
wanted a sophisticated stationery
system that her own clients, designers and art directors, would respond
to. This elegant, all-type treatment
fits the bill nicely.
Special Visual Effects A closer look
at the logo rewards the viewer with a
number of writing-related epigrams.
Cost $3,000
Initial Print Run 2,500

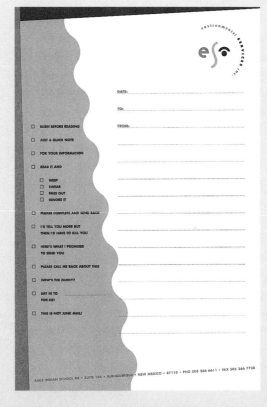

Art Director/Studio Brenda Kilmer/
Kilmer, Kilmer & James Inc.
Designer/Studio Randall Marshall/
Kilmer, Kilmer & James Inc
Client/Service Environmental
Services Inc./environmental
consultation
Paper Simpson Starwhite Vicksburg
Type Garamond, Garamond Italic,
Futura Bold (title); Futura Bold
(address)
Colors Three, match
Printing Offset
Software Adobe Illustrator,
QuarkXPress
Billable Hours to Complete 12
Concept The playfulness of this sys-
tem—a vibrant color scheme and the
initials of the company forming a
face for the logo—is meant to reflect
the spirit of the client, which
describes itself as an "environmen-
tally friendly company." The logo
also reflects the client's function—
keeping an eye on the environment.
Cost $4,500
Initial Print Run 2,000

Art Directors/Studio Jeff Fabian,
Sam Shelton/KINETIK
Communications Graphics, Inc.
Designer/Studio Mimi Massé/
KINETIK Communications
Graphics, Inc.
Illustrator Mimi Massé
Client/Service Tropical Express/
restaurant and juice bar
Paper Gilbert ESSE
Type Meta Plus, Quartet Small Caps
Colors Two, match
Printing Offset
Software QuarkXPress, Aldus
FreeHand

Concept The client wanted an identity that would call attention to the fact
that they had something unique to
offer, compared to competing lunch
spots in the downtown area. This
bright and dynamic system suggests
the healthy fare that sets the client
apart from the competition.
Special Visual Effects The use of
fruit as type on the back of the business cards demonstrates the design
firm's attention to detail.
Initial Print Run 1,000

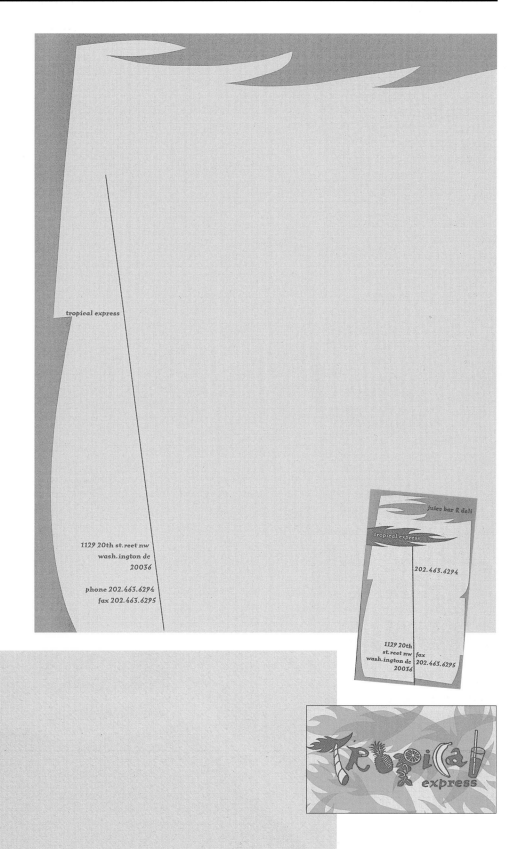

Art Director/Studio Kam Wai Yu/
Two Dimensions Inc.
Designer/Studio Phouvieng Sackda/
Two Dimensions Inc.
Client/Service The Persona
Principle/image marketing
Paper Neenah Classic Columns
Type Epoka (logo), Helvetica
(address)
Colors Two, process
Printing Offset
Software Adobe Illustrator
Billable Hours to Complete 20

Concept To promote the image-
marketing firm run by this design
studio, the designers used a simple
but playful type treatment and a two-
color print job. To play off the left-
brain/right-brain dynamic of the two
partners in the firm, one partner's
business card is printed with one
side of the logo, while the other's is
printed with the other side.
Cost $3,200

Art Director/Studio Toni Schowalter/
Toni Schowalter Design
Designer/Studio Toni Schowalter/
Toni Schowalter Design
Client/Service Marshall Watson
Interiors/interior design
Paper Strathmore Writing Wove
Natural
Type Bodoni, Bauer Bodoni
Colors Two, match
Printing Offset
Software QuarkXPress

Concept This traditional letterhead
design works well for the client, an
interior decorator who specializes in
design with a Victorian feel.
Special Visual Effects The pattern
used as a motif throughout the system resembles the types of fabric
patterns the client favors in his work.
Initial Print Run 1,000

Sharon Boguch, Producer
2351 31st Avenue South
Seattle, WA 98144
Phone 206.725.9763
Fax 206.725.9716
E-mail snb@halcyon.com

Art Director/Studio Pat Hansen/ Hansen Design Company
Designer/Studio Pat Hansen/Hansen Design Company
Client/Service Sharon Boguch/commercial television producer
Paper Gilbert ESSE Bright White
Type Sabon, Franklin Gothic Condensed
Colors Two, black and match
Printing Offset
Software Aldus FreeHand
Billable Hours to Complete 18.5

Concept As a producer, the client is required to orchestrate many different elements, to bring "order out of chaos." This concept is typographically illustrated through a series of letters, first in a jumble and then more and more organized down the side of each piece.
Cost-Cutting Techniques Smaller notepaper was created by trimming an overrun of the letterhead.
Special Visual Effects The tan ink color mimicking Kraft paper gives the system a look that's "hands-on" but sophisticated, but printing it on bright white paper gives the system an orderly feel.
Cost $3,500 (design and production); $1,150 (printing)
Initial Print Run 1,000

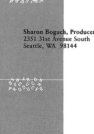

Art Director/Studio Steve Wedeen/
Vaughn/Wedeen Creative
Designers/Studio Steve Wedeen,
Lucy Hitchcock/Vaughn/Wedeen
Creative
Illustrator Vivian Harder
Client/Service US West Home and
Personal Services/telecommunica-
tions
Paper Cross Pointe Genesis Husk
Writing
Type Koloss, Coronet
Colors Four, process
Printing Offset
Software QuarkXPress, Aldus
FreeHand

Concept To promote the company's
in-house sales promotion, in which
the top salesperson won a trip to a
dude ranch, this letterhead used type
and color to carry through this
Western theme. The whimsical illustration of "Lucky Lil" on the horse
was meant to underscore the tag line
of the competition: "Kick up your
heels."
Initial Print Run 5,000

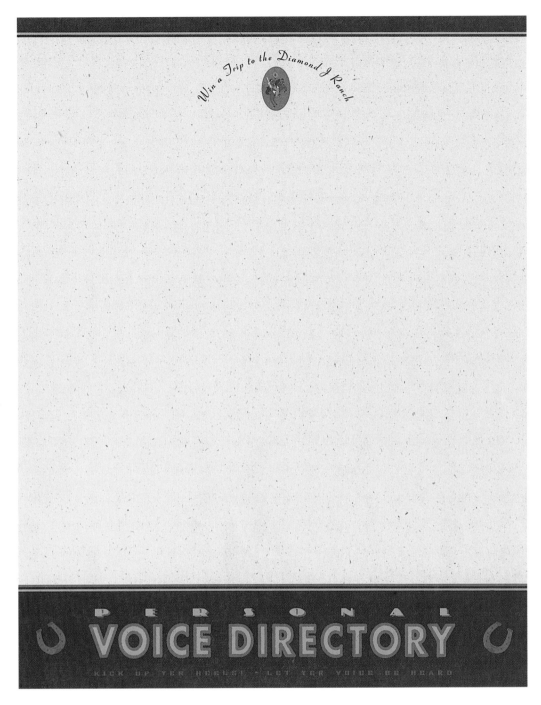

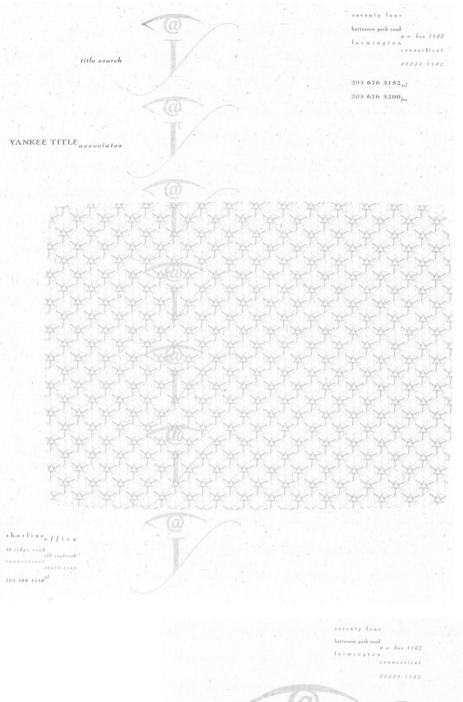

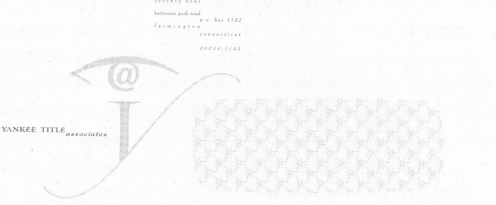

Designer/Studio Shawn Coulter/
Coulter Design
Client/Service Yankee Title
Associates/real estate title search
Paper Strathmore Ivorystone Laid
Type Bernhard Roman
Colors Two, match
Printing Offset
Software Adobe Illustrator,
QuarkXPress

Concept Type and layout are
employed to get maximum effect at
a minimal cost in this system for a
client who performs real estate title
searches.
Cost $2,100
Initial Print Run 1,500

Art Director/Studio Tracy Holdeman/
Love Packaging Group
Designers/Studio Tracy Holdeman,
Brian Miller/Love Packaging Group
Client/Service Love Packaging
Group/design firm specializing in
packaging
Paper Strathmore Elements
Type Bank Gothic, Bureau Agency
Colors Two, black and match
Printing Offset
Software Aldus FreeHand
Billable Hours to Complete 6
(design), 17 (production)

Concept To end the misconception
that Love Packaging Group, which is
a division of a corrugated packaging
manufacturer, only did "this-end-
up"-caliber graphics, the designers
came up with this streamlined yet
up-to-the-minute solution. The logo
itself, with a box standing in for the
pupil in an eye, suggests creative
vision in packaging. The abundance
of rules, the lined paper stock and the
color scheme all refer to the division's parent company without making an issue of it.
Cost $3,000
Initial Print Run 2,000 for most
pieces, 500 each name (business
card)

[in·sync] the customer and you

[in·sync]

Together.

Be friendly.

Art Director/Studio Rick Vaughn/
Vaughn/Wedeen Creative
Designer/Studio Rick Vaughn/
Vaughn/Wedeen Creative
Photographer Michael Barley
Client/Service US West Small
Business Group/telecommunications
Paper Neenah Classic Crest
Recycled Bright White
Type Courier, Gill Sans
Colors Four, process
Printing Offset
Software QuarkXPress, Adobe
Photoshop, Aldus FreeHand

Concept The designers of this system used three primary design elements to convey their client's com-
mitment to customer/employee
teamwork: a gear motif, a variety of
motivational words used as a background texture and a composite shot
of six individuals.
Special Production Techniques To
create the composite image, six different people were photographed in
black and white, from the same angle
and to scale, and various pieces of
each photograph were painstakingly
assembled into one image in
Photoshop.
Initial Print Run 10,000

SMALL

BUSINESS

GROUP

[in·sync] the customer and you

NEXTLINK™

NEXTLINK™

155 108th Avenue NE
8th Floor
Bellevue, WA 98004

155 108th Ave. NE
8th Floor
Bellevue, WA 98004
206.519.8900
fax: 206.519.8910

NEXTLINK™

155 108th Ave. NE
8th Floor
Bellevue, WA 98004
206.519.8905

NEXTLINK™

Christen Jeans
Staff Accountant

155 108th Ave. NE, 8th Fl.
Bellevue, WA 98004

206.519.8937
1.800.701.8207
fax: 206.519.8910

Art Director/Studio Jack Anderson/ Hornall Anderson Design Works
Designers/Studio Jack Anderson, David Bates, Mary Hermes, John Anicker, Larry Anderson, Mary Chin Hutchison/Hornall Anderson Design Works
Client/Service NextLink/full-service telecommunications provider
Paper Neenah Classic Crest
Type Custom
Colors Four, process
Printing Offset
Software Adobe Photoshop, Aldus FreeHand, QuarkXPress

Concept This system, created to capitalize upon the client's name change, uses an innovative typographic solution and color treatment to communicate the forward-thinking nature of the firm, which specializes in the next wave of telecommunications services.
Special Visual Effects The change in color of the logotype from left to right suggests the evolving nature of the client's business.

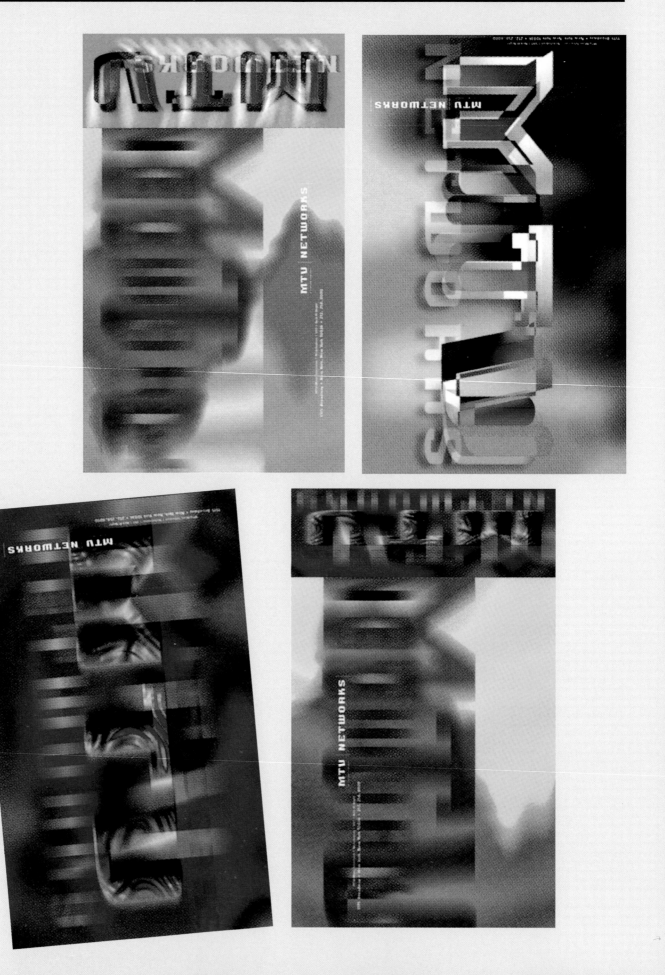

Art Director/Studio Carlos Segura/
Segura Inc.
Designer/Studio Carlos Segura/
Segura Inc.
Illustrators Hatch Letterpress, Tony
Klassen
Client/Service MTV/television
network
Paper Various
Type Letterpress, Werkman
Colors Four, process
Printing Offset, letterpress
Software Adobe Photoshop,
QuarkXPress

Concept These eight type treatments,
developed for the back of MTV's
stationery system, work well to suggest the client's cutting-edge image.

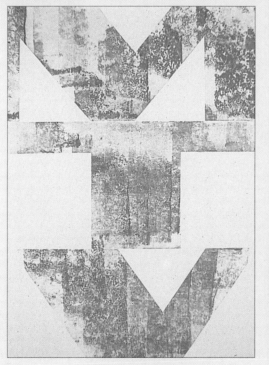

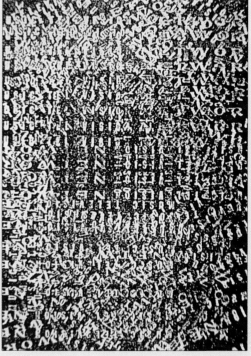

Art Director/Studio Takaaki
Matsumoto/Matsumoto Incorporated
Designer/Studio Takaaki
Matsumoto/Matsumoto Incorporated
Client/Service Michael Maharam/
personal stationery
Paper Crane Crest
Type Futura
Colors Two, match
Printing Engraving
Software QuarkXPress

Concept This all-type solution uses a
fresh color scheme and an unusual
layout for a unique but subtle look.
Special Production Techniques The
use of engraving gives the type a
richer feel.
Initial Print Run 2,000

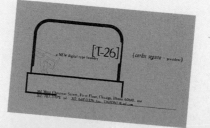

Art Director/Studio Carlos Segura/
Segura Inc.
Designer/Studio Carlos Segura/
Segura Inc.
Client/Service [T-26]/type foundry
Paper Gilbert ESSE
Type Tema Cantante
Colors Two, process
Printing Offset
Software QuarkXPress, Adobe
Illustrator

Concept An elegant type treatment,
combined with a three-dimensional
all-type logo, conveys both the spirit
and the business of this type foundry.
The blurred type treatment on the
back of the letterhead and business
cards conveys the nature of the type
foundry's business without favoring
any specific typeface.
Special Visual Effects The reversed-
out type on the back of the business
cards allows the variety of paper colors used for the cards to lend different colors to the type.
Initial Print Run 5,000

Special Production Techniques

Since letterhead is one of the most rule-bound pieces to design, with the realities of the post office and the typewriter (and now the laser printer) all constraining design choices, it's in the details that designers strive to make their letterhead systems stand out from the crowd. That accounts for the popularity of special production techniques such as die cuts, varnishes, engraving and the like in the world of letterhead and business card design: How better to design a piece that's unusual, yet still usable and sendable?

It's special touches like these that set the systems in this chapter apart from other letterhead systems. Some of these details, such as a system that's been printed by letterpress, are so subtle that they can only be discerned if you hold the piece in your hands; others, such as an unusual die cut, immediately catch your attention. But all show an attention to detail that separates the great solution from the merely adequate one.

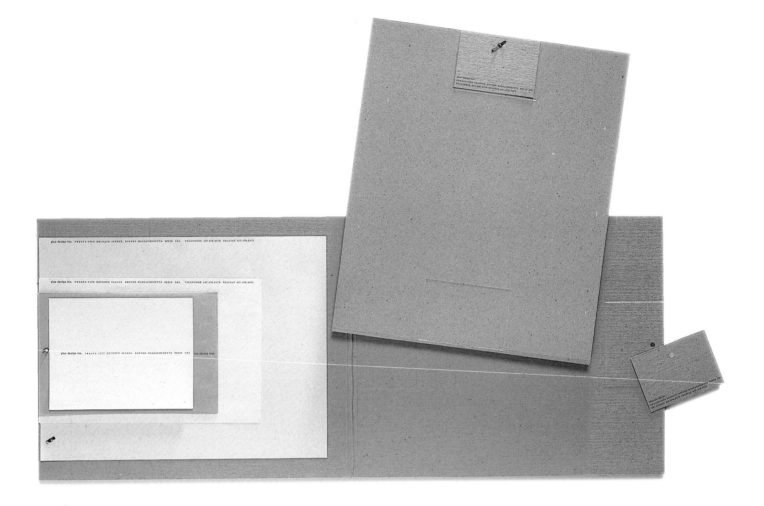

Art Director/Studio Anita Meyer, Karin Fickett/plus design inc.

Designers/Studio Anita Meyer, Karin Fickett, Dina Zaccagnini, Matthew Monk, Nicole Juen, Carolina Senior, Veronica Majlona/plus design inc.

Client/Service plus design inc./design

Paper French Newsprint White (letterhead), French Butcher White (memo sheet), French Primer Gold (envelope), French Chipboard (business card, folder)

Type Letter Gothic (plus design woodmark), Bauer Bodoni (address)

Colors One, match

Printing Letterpress

Software QuarkXPress, Adobe Illustrator

Concept To communicate their philosophy of avoiding the imposition of a preconceived design style on their projects, this design firm developed a subtle but exquisitely detailed system. The use of a muted type and color treatment ensures that the myriad of extra printing touches, including die cutting, hole-punching, embossing and debossing, letterpress and the use of recycled cardboard, takes center stage. The entire presentation folder and letterhead system fit together in a way that underscores this attention to detail.

Initial Print Run 5,000

SAGMEISTER INC.

NEW YORK

STYLE = FART

SAGMEISTER INC.

222 WEST 14th STREET NEW YORK NY 10011 US of A TEL (212) 647 1789 FAX (212) 647 1788

Art Director/Studio Stefan
Sagmeister/Sagmeister Inc.

Designer/Studio Stefan Sagmeister/
Sagmeister Inc.

Illustrator Karin Kautzky

Client/Service Sagmeister Inc./
graphic design

Paper Strathmore Writing

Type Spartan

Colors One, black

Printing Offset

Software QuarkXPress, Adobe
Illustrator

Concept A simple, easy-to-reproduce
logo is jazzed up when used in conjunction with acetate; the business
card remains mysterious until the

recipient slides the card out of its
acetate holder, to reveal the name and
address of the designer.

Special Production Techniques All
business cards were assembled by
hand.

Special Visual Effects On the back of
the letterhead, the design studio's
logo is rendered in vertical stripes

and is only completed when the sheet
is folded and wrapped by a band of
acetate, where the logo is also rendered in vertical stripes; sliding off
the acetate band produces a unique
doubling effect of the logo.

Initial Print Run 1,000

Art Director/Studio Rita Marshall/
Delessert and Marshall
Designer/Studio Rita Marshall/
Delessert and Marshall
Illustrator Etienne Delessert
Client/Service The Creative
Company/children's book publisher
Paper Crane Crest
Type Belucian (logo, copy);
Kuenstler Script (logo initials)
Colors Four, process, and one, match
Printing Offset with die cut
Software QuarkXPress

Concept To succinctly communicate
the nature of the client's business, the
designer created a die-cut minibook
with the traditional contact information on one side of the "spread" and
the logo of the company on the other.
Initial Print Run 5,000

Art Director/Studio Rita Marshall/
Delessert and Marshall
Designer/Studio Rita Marshall/
Delessert and Marshall
Illustrators Etienne Delessert (*I Hate
to Read*), Monique Felix (*Opposites*),
Gary Kelley (*The Necklace*)
Client/Service The Creative
Company/children's book publisher
Paper Hopper Cardigan
Type Kabel Condensed
Colors Four, process, and one, black
Printing Offset

Concept The designer of this system
came up with a clever way both to
communicate the nature of the
client's business—children's
books—and to promote its product:
four-color "minibook" stickers that
can be updated as needed to promote
the client's latest publications.
Initial Print Run 5,000

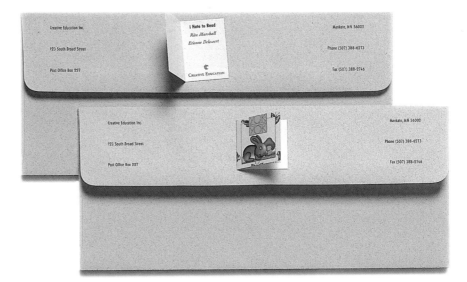

Art Directors/Studio Silvio Silva
Junior, Karine Mitsui Kawamura/
Studio Lúmen
Designers/Studio Silvio Silva Junior,
Karine Mitsui Kawamura/Studio
Lúmen
Client/Service Felissimo/fast food
Type Custom design (logotype),
hand-lettering
Colors Three, black and match
Printing Offset
Software CorelDRAW, Adobe
Streamline
Billable Hours to Complete 19
(senior designer), 24 (junior design-
er), 16 (trainee)

Concept In Portuguese, "felissimo"
means happiness; the playful colors,
hand-lettering and illustration rein-
force this feeling in this system for a
fast-food restaurant.
Cost $10,250

Art Director/Studio John Sayles/
Sayles Graphic Design
Designer/Studio John Sayles/Sayles
Graphic Design
Illustrator John Sayles
Client/Service The Finishing Touch/
finishing (labeling, gluing, packaging, etc.)
Paper Incentive (letterhead), Kraft
Policy (envelope), Springhill Manila
(business card)
Type Franklin Gothic Extra
Condensed
Colors One, match (each
piece)
Printing Offset with rubber
stamp and adhesive labels

Concept This letterhead system for a
finishing service communicates the
nature of the client's services by
employing these services abundantly
throughout.
Special Production Techniques The
letterhead includes a miniature shipping tag rubber stamped with a list
of services and applied with an eyelet. The address is rubber stamped
on both the envelope and the business card. The business card also
includes a handmade plastic label
with the employee's name and a
decorative plastic star hand glued
to each card.
Cost-Cutting Techniques
Individual components are printed in one color. All the
"enhancements" are inexpensive
stock items. Since their business
is handwork, employees can
assemble the components of
their letterhead during downtime
Initial Print Run 1,000

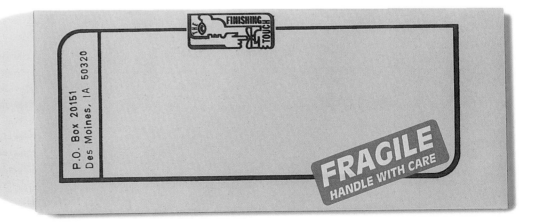

Art Director/Studio William T. Kochi/Kode Associates, Inc.
Designer/Studio William T. Kochi/ Kode Associates, Inc.
Client/Service Kode Associates, Inc./design communications
Paper Gilbert Oxford Cream
Type Minion
Colors Three, black and match
Printing Offset with engraving
Software Adobe Illustrator

Concept To solve the problem most designers have when designing their own letterhead—how do you design a letterhead that's creative enough to show off your design skills but neutral enough that it won't turn off more conservative clients?—this letterhead combines simple typography and creative type placement and a neutral, though current, color scheme with a uniquely placed blind emboss.
Special Visual Effects Taking advantage of the fact that the studio name, typed in capital letters (KODE), is symmetrical when divided horizontally, the blind emboss of the name is placed so that it appears to wrap around the edge of each component of the system.
Cost $2,500
Initial Print Run 10,000 (first and second sheets), 5,000 (envelope), 1,000 (business card)

Art Director/Studio Rick Eiber/Rick Eiber Design (RED)
Designer/Studio Rick Eiber/Rick Eiber Design (RED)
Illustrator Gary Volk
Client/Service On the Wall/painting contractor
Paper French Speckletone
Type Didot modified (logo)
Colors Two over one, black and match
Printing Offset
Software Adobe Photoshop, Adobe Illustrator
Billable Hours to Complete 16

Concept Taking the name of this painting contractor back to its cave-painting origins twenty thousand years ago, this system conveys the artistry of On the Wall's work.
Special Production Techniques The logo is printed as a black and metallic duotone.
Special Visual Effects Each business card is printed on the back with the hand and signature of the painter whom the card is for, giving each business card a unique personal touch. The interior of the envelope is printed so that it looks like a pair of hands is reaching out to the recipient.
Cost $4,740
Initial Print Run 2,000

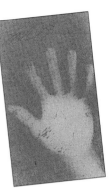
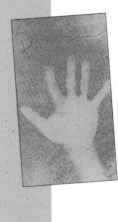
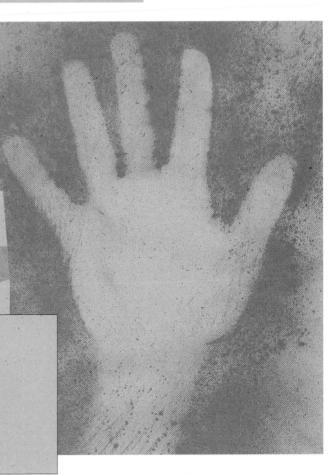

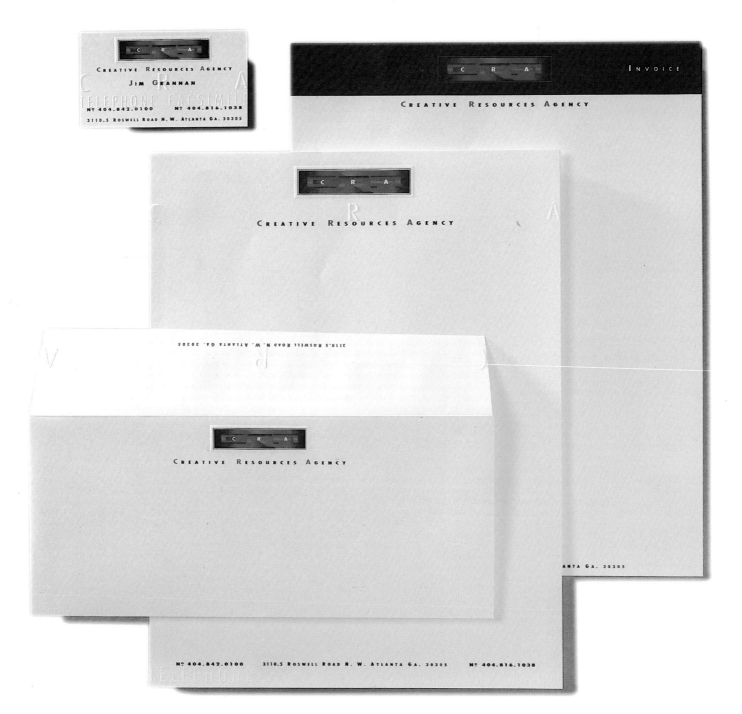

Art Directors/Studio Tom Antista, Thomas Fairclough/Antista Fairclough Design

Designers/Studio Tom Antista, Thomas Fairclough/Antista Fairclough Design

Client/Service Creative Resources Agency/creative resources

Type Futura Condensed

Colors Four, match, plus varnish

Printing Offset with embossing

Software Adobe Illustrator

Billable Hours to Complete 12-15

Concept The simplicity of the color scheme and type treatment on this letterhead system for a creative resources agency allows the system to work for corporate clients of the firm, but the innovative use of embossing and the current type treatment in the logo allow the system to work for the creatives within these firms.

Initial Print Run 1,000

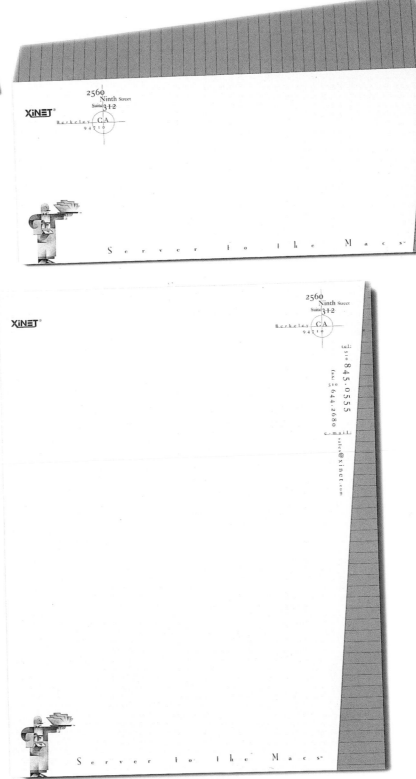

Art Director/Studio Earl Gee/Gee +
Chung Design

Designer/Studio Earl Gee/Gee +
Chung Design

Illustrator Robert Pastrana

Client/Service Xinet/Macintosh and
Unix server software for the electronic prepress market

Paper Simpson Starwhite Vicksburg
Bright White (letterhead, envelope);
Potlatch Quintessence (business card)

Type Caslon 540 (address), Mona
Lisa Solid (tag line), OCR-A (marketing messages)

Colors Four, process, plus one, match

Printing Offset

Software QuarkXPress, Adobe
Illustrator, Adobe Photoshop

Billable Hours to Complete 30

Concept The designer of this system
used an abundance of design elements
to convey the client's rather abstract
product: prepress software that shares
files between Macintosh and Unix
computers. The illustration of a
"server" used throughout the system
conveys the product's function in a
down-to-earth manner; the typographic arrangement of the address
references a printer's registration
mark. The business card and back of
the letterhead verbally convey marketing messages and product benefits.

Special Production Techniques The
die-cut business card forms an X (for

Xinet) when closed; the angled flap
on the envelope alludes to the angles
of the product packaging.

Initial Print Run 15,000 (letterhead,
envelope); 500 each of 20 names
(business card)

Art Director/Studio Silvio Silva Junior/Studio Lúmen

Designer/Studio Silvio Silva Junior/ Studio Lúmen

Client/Service Sérgio Sossélla/ fashion photography

Type Custom design (logotype), Futura

Colors Two over one, match

Printing Offset

Software CorelDRAW

Billable Hours to Complete 20 (senior designer), 16 (junior designer), 12 (trainee)

Concept To reflect the open-minded spirit of the client, a fashion photographer, this all-type solution is a simple but fashion-forward look. The use of a number of different stickers allows the photographer flexibility in the use of his identity.

Special Production Techniques The business card and envelope are die-cut.

Cost $4,641

Art Directors/Studio Kristin Sommese, Lanny Sommese/ Sommese Design
Designer/Studio Kristin Sommese/ Sommese Design
Illustrator Lanny Sommese
Client/Service AquaPenn Spring Water Company/spring water products
Paper Monadnock Astrolite Brilliant White
Type Industria
Colors One, match
Printing Offset
Software Aldus PageMaker
Billable Hours to Complete 5

Concept The combination of an ink color suggestive of water and printed on bright white paper stock and a clear, rounded die cut gives this system a visual purity equivalent to the purity of the client's product—spring water.
Special Production Techniques All pieces were embossed, and the business card was die cut.
Cost $1,524 (not including logo design, which Sommese Design designed previously)
Initial Print Run 1,000 (letterhead, envelope); 500 (business card)

AquaPenn spring water company

P.O. Box 938, One AquaPenn Drive, Milesburg, Pennsylvania 16853, Phone 814. 355. 5556, Fax 814. 355.7810

AquaPenn spring water company

Edward J. Lauth, III
President

P.O. Box 938
One AquaPenn Drive
Milesburg
Pennsylvania 16853
Phone
814. 355. 5556
Extension 111

AquaPenn spring water company

P.O. Box 938
One AquaPenn Drive
Milesburg
Pennsylvania 16853

Art Director/Studio Takaaki Matsumoto/Matsumoto Incorporated
Designer/Studio Takaaki Matsumoto/Matsumoto Incorporated
Client/Service Pen Plus Inc./ communications consultation
Paper Crane Crest
Type Univers
Colors One, match
Printing Engraving
Software QuarkXPress

Concept For this Japanese communications consulting firm, the combination of embossing and fluorescent ink communicates the client's business philosophy, which likewise combines the time-tested and the timely.
Initial Print Run 2,000

Studio After Hours Creative

Photographer Arthur Holeman

Client/Service Culinary Arts and Entertainment/food-related special events and dining guides

Paper Neenah Classic Crest Recycled Natural White

Type Tasse Condensed

Colors Two, black and match

Printing Offset

Software Adobe Illustrator, Adobe Photoshop

Billable Hours to Complete 100-150

Concept To come up with an accessible but upscale look that reflects the food-related nature of the client's business, the designer used a cafe sign whose burnt-out letter "F" allowed the sign to read as the client's acronym—"CAE". The mark instantly communicates dining, along with a classy yet down-to-earth feel.

Special Production Techniques The cafe sign was actually created and photographed for the purpose of this letterhead—burnt-out letter "F" and all.

Cost $5,000

Initial Print Run 1,000

culinary arts & entertainment

7610 e. mcdonald dr. suite h, scottsdale, az 85250

tel: 602 998 5810   tel: 800 211 5844   fax: 602 998 9064

culinary arts & entertainment
7610 e. mcdonald dr. suite h
scottsdale, az 85250

culinary arts & entertainment
7610 e. mcdonald dr. suite h
scottsdale, az 85250
tel: 602 998 5810
tel: 800 211 5844
fax: 602 998 9064
karl d. roessler

Art Director/Studio Sonia Greteman/
Greteman Group
Designers/Studio Sonia Greteman,
James Strange/Greteman Group
Client/Service Perfectly Round
Productions/film and video services
Paper Beckett Concept Natural
Cream
Type Franklin Gothic
Colors Two, match
Printing Offset
Software Aldus FreeHand
Billable Hours to Complete 24

Concept A depiction of a square
object with a round shadow and a
halo serves both as an unexpected
interpretation of the company's
name and as the visual centerpiece
of this system for a film and video
service.
Special Production Techniques A
full bleed of the second green color
with a 70 percent tint worked well
with the green tint of the paper, providing subtle type treatments to
communicate additional services.
All the film was ganged together on
one sheet; a pre-existing die cut was
used for the converted envelope.
Budget $3,000
Initial Print Run 5,000

Art Director/Studio Petrula Vrontikis/Vrontikis Design Office
Designer/Studio Kim Sage/Vrontikis Design Office
Client/Service Jacksons/restaurant
Paper French Dur-o-tone (letterhead), French Speckletone (envelope), Beveridge placard posterboard (business card)
Type Matrix (address), hand-lettering (logo)
Colors One, match
Printing Letterpress
Software QuarkXPress, Adobe Photoshop
Billable Hours to Complete 20

Concept Rough-hewn hand-lettering and an earthy color scheme are combined in a simple, direct representation of the client's restaurant concept: the feel of the American prairie conveyed in a sophisticated way.
Special Production Techniques Manipulation with a photocopier created the texture in the logo. Printing with letterpress accentuated this texture, especially on the posterboard used for the business card.
Cost $5,000
Initial Print Run 5,000

Art Director/Studio John Ball/Mires Design, Inc.

Designers/Studio John Ball, Miguel Perez/Mires Design, Inc.

Client/Service Mires Design, Inc./ graphic design

Paper Gilbert Correspond

Type Franklin Gothic Extra Bold

Colors Two, black and match

Printing Letterpress

Software Adobe Illustrator

Concept This design firm wanted a stationery system that was unusual yet timeless. Choosing the thickest paper stock they could find and printing it with a hand-fed letterpress gave this system the strong, unique feel the firm wanted.

Special Production Techniques Rounded, die-cut edges give the business card an unusual extra touch.

Cost $7,000

Initial Print Run 4,000 (letterhead, envelope); 2,000 (business card)

MIRES DESIGN INC

2345 KETTNER BLVD SAN DIEGO CA 92101

PHONE: 619 234 6631 FAX: 619 234 1807

MIRES DESIGN INC

2345 KETTNER BLVD SAN DIEGO CA 92101

PHONE: 619 234 6631 FAX: 619 234 1807

E MAIL: MIRES@MIRESDESIGN.COM

SCOTT MIRES

MIRES DESIGN INC

2345 KETTNER BOULEVARD

SAN DIEGO CALIFORNIA 92101

Art Director/Studio Takaaki
Matsumoto/Matsumoto Incorporated
Designer/Studio Takaaki
Matsumoto/Matsumoto Incorporated
Client/Service I Pezzi Dipinti/
custom-made furniture importer
Paper Crane Crest
Type Copperplate
Colors Two, match
Printing Offset with engraving
Software Adobe Illustrator,
QuarkXPress

Concept To refer to the client's business—importing handmade furniture
based on eighteenth-century Italian
designs—the color palette is meant
to imitate a patina.
Special Production Techniques
Engraving adds to the rich look of
the system.
Initial Print Run 2,000

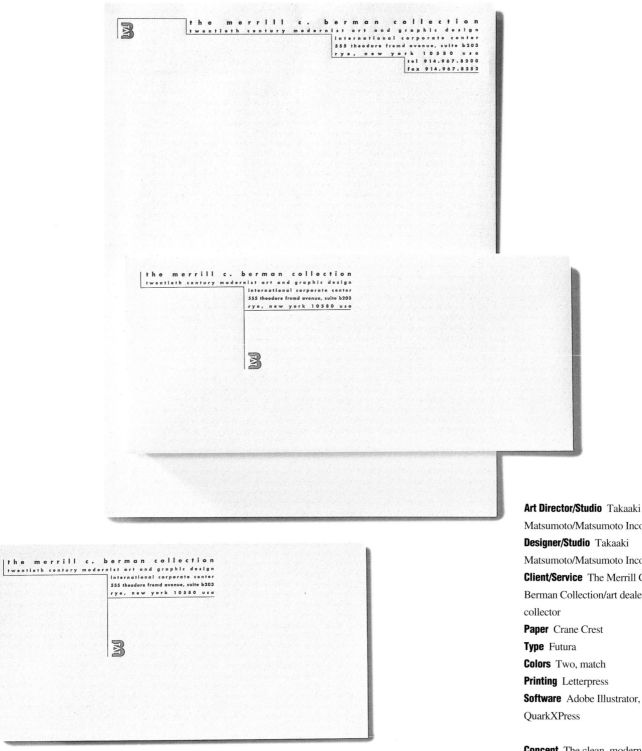

Art Director/Studio Takaaki Matsumoto/Matsumoto Incorporated
Designer/Studio Takaaki Matsumoto/Matsumoto Incorporated
Client/Service The Merrill C. Berman Collection/art dealer and collector
Paper Crane Crest
Type Futura
Colors Two, match
Printing Letterpress
Software Adobe Illustrator, QuarkXPress

Concept The clean, modern look of this system is appropriate for a collection of modern art and graphic design. The typographic logo is equally streamlined, and just as fitting.
Special Production Techniques The use of letterpress gives this system a more tactile appeal.
Initial Print Run 2,000

Art Director/Studio Petrula Vrontikis/
Vrontikis Design Office
Designer/Studio Kim Sage/Vrontikis
Design Office
Client/Service Hasegawa Enterprise
Ltd./restaurant
Paper Neenah Classic Crest
Type Matrix (address), hand-lettering
(logo)

Colors Three, match
Printing Offset
Software QuarkXPress, Adobe
Photoshop
Billable Hours to Complete 40

Concept The patterns and textures
used throughout this system were
drawn from the elaborate imagery

used in the restaurant for which it
was designed.
Special Production Techniques A
symbol from the identity is reversed
out of a full-bleed metallic on the
back of the letterhead, mimicking the
effect of a watermark from the front.
Special Visual Effects In an unusual
handling of the need for the business

card to be in English and in Japanese,
the business card uses exactly the
same layout on both sides, with the
text being Japanese on one side and
English on the other.
Cost $10,000
Initial Print Run 8,000

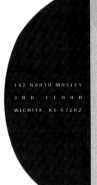

Art Directors/Studio Sonia Greteman, James Strange/Greteman Group
Designers/Studio Sonia Greteman, James Strange/Greteman Group
Client/Service Greteman Group/ design
Paper Strathmore Renewal Moss
Type Franklin Gothic Exocet
Colors Four, match
Printing Offset
Software Aldus FreeHand
Billable Hours to Complete 24

Concept This sophisticated system is an intriguing juxtaposition of opposites: Curved die cuts contrast with linear graphics and modern typefaces contrast with a Gothic typeface.
Special Production Techniques A tint varnish was used on the uncoated paper for a subtle screened look. A screen of the burgundy was used under the black ink to emulate a double hit of black. A standing die was used for the rounded side envelope flap.
Budget $3,000
Initial Print Run 5,000

115 stuart street   city place   boston massachusetts 02116
telephone 617-742-5225   telefax 617-742-6620

Art Director/Studio Anita Meyer/plus design inc.
Designer/Studio Anita Meyer/plus design inc.
Client/Service Brew Moon Enterprises/restaurant and micro-brewery
Paper Hopper Proterra Fleck Chalk
Type New Gothic Condensed Bold and Regular
Colors Three, match
Printing Offset
Software QuarkXPress, Adobe Illustrator, Adobe Photoshop

Concept The attention to detail exhibited in this die-cut letterhead system suggests the quality of the client's handcrafted beer and imaginative menu. The "brew" portion of the name is robustly rendered in gray type, while the "moon" portion of the name appears in a whimsical purple script.
Special Visual Effects The laser die cutting used to etch out the word "brew" in the logotype creates a burnt brown effect around the letters on the back of the letterhead and business card—an appropriately rugged effect.
Initial Print Run 5,000 (letterhead, business card); 20,000 (envelope); 3,000 (mailing label)

115 stuart street   city place   boston massachusetts 02116

Mark G. Bennett **general manager**
115 stuart street   city place   boston massachusetts 02116
telephone 617-742-5225   telefax 617-742-6620

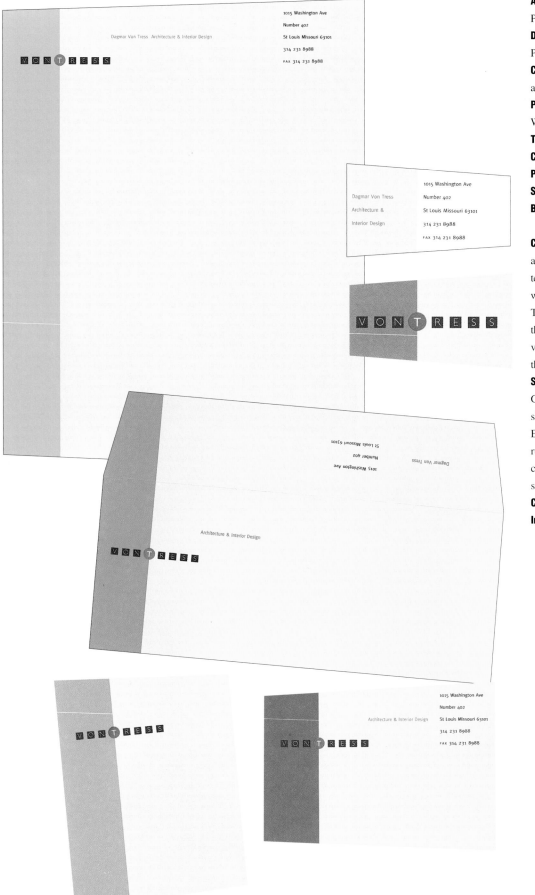

Art Director/Studio Eric Thoelke/
Phoenix Creative
Designer/Studio Eric Thoelke/
Phoenix Creative
Client/Service Dagmar Von Tress/
architecture and interior design
Paper Strathmore Bright White
Writing
Type Gill Sans (logo), Meta
Colors Four, black and match
Printing Offset
Software QuarkXPress
Billable Hours to Complete 35

Concept An angular motif seemed
an appropriate solution for an architect and interior designer whose
work does not rely on right angles.
The playfulness and movement of
the client's work is reflected in the
variety of shapes and colors used in
this system.
Special Production Techniques
Guillotine cuts provided an inexpensive alternative to full die cutting.
Each different paper stock form was
run on a six-color press to maximize
color hits while keeping costs reasonable.
Cost $5,000
Initial Print Run 5,000

Art Director/Studio Stefan
Sagmeister/Sagmeister Inc.
Designers/Studio Veronica Oh,
Stefan Sagmeister/Sagmeister Inc.
Illustrator Veronica Oh
Photographer Tom Schierlitz
Client/Service Naked Music/music
production
Paper Strathmore Writing
Type Rotis
Colors Three, process
Printing Offset
Software Adobe Photoshop, Adobe
Illustrator

Concept The central photograph
used on this system takes the client's
name, Naked Music, to its most
extreme interpretation. The tongue-
in-cheek concept, combined with an
up-to-the-minute metallic color
scheme, communicates an appropriately hip image for this music-busi-
ness client.
Special Production Techniques
Metallic inks were substituted for
process colors.
Initial Print Run 1,500

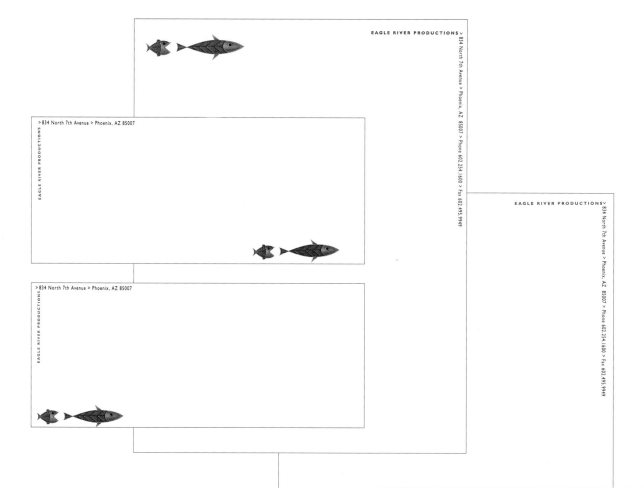

Studio John Brady Design Consultants, Inc.

Illustrator Frank Frisari

Client/Service Eagle River Communications/marketing communications

Paper Strathmore Writing Ultimate White Laid (letterhead, second sheet, envelope); MacTac Starliner Blinding White (mailing label)

Type Gill Sans

Colors Four, process, plus one, match

Printing Offset

Software QuarkXPress

Concept To convey the small but aggressive nature of this company, a motif of a small fish chasing after a big fish was created. This system was designed to coordinate with the client's two sister companies; all three companies share the same cor-porate logo and identity, but each has a different match color added to its system.

Cost-Cutting Techniques The four-color fish image was preprinted on the entire print run for all three companies, with a separate match ink for each company added in the second print run.

Initial Print Run 2,000 each for 3 companies (letterhead, second sheet); 250 per company (business card); 1,000 per company (mailing label, envelope)

Copyright Notices

All images have been reproduced with the knowledge and consent of the artists concerned.

P. 18 © Vaughn/Wedeen Creative.
P. 19 © Segura Inc.
P. 20 © 1989 Douglas May Design, Inc.
P. 21 © 1995 Rock and Roll Hall of Fame and Museum.
P. 22 © Vaughn/Wedeen Creative.
P. 23 © Sagmeister Inc.
P. 24 © 1995 The Bradford Lawton Design Group.
P. 25 © 1995 Belyea Design Alliance.
P. 26 © 1995 TeamDesign, Inc.
P. 27 © 1995 Gee + Chung Design.
P. 28 © Sagmeister Inc.
P. 29 © Segura Inc.
P. 30 © 1995 Sayles Graphic Design.
P. 30 © 1995 Rick Eiber and Richard Kehl.
P. 30 © Tarzan Communications Inc.
P. 31 © Global Investment Concept, Inc., Kozo Hasegawa.
P. 32 © 1994 Baby Bookworms Stationery.
P. 33 © Mike Salisbury Communications.
P. 34 © Vaughn/Wedeen Creative.
P. 35 © Dyer/Mutchnick Group, Inc.
P. 36 © 1995 Greteman Group.
P. 37 © The Georgian Hotel, Santa Monica, California.
P. 38 © Sackett Design Associates, San Francisco/ Kansas City.
P. 39 © KINETIK Communications Graphics, Inc.
P. 40 © Vaughn/Wedeen Creative.
P. 41 © Tarzan Communications Inc.
P. 42 © GE Capital Assurance and Hornall Anderson Design Works, Inc.
P. 43 © Pierson Hawkins Inc. Advertising.
P. 44 © Mires Design.
P. 45 © Pacific Coast Feather Company and Hornall Anderson Design Works, Inc.
P. 46 © Studio Lúmen.
P. 47 © 1995 Greteman Group.
P. 48 © KINETIK Communications Graphics, Inc.
P. 49 © 1995 Acumen Group.
P. 50 © 1995 Greteman Group.
P. 51 © Capons Rotisserie Chicken and Hornall Anderson Design Works, Inc.
P. 54 © Swieter Design USA.
P. 55 © Eric Kass Design.
P. 56 © Tarzan Communications Inc.
P. 57 © Studio MD, Inc.
P. 58 © Paula Sloane/Callahan and Co.
P. 59 © 1995 Hal Apple Design, Inc.
P. 60 © Masi Graphica Ltd.
P. 61 © DogStar.
P. 62 © Eric Kass Design.
P. 63 © 1995 Rick Eiber Design.
P. 64 © Lanny Sommese.
P. 64 © 1995 Industrial Strength Design.
P. 65 © 1995 Reuter Design and Donna Schumaker.
P. 66 © Nicholas Associates.
P. 67 © Vaughn/Wedeen Creative.
P. 68 © Lance Anderson Design.
P. 69 © 1995 Industrial Strength Design.
P. 69 © Love Packaging Group.
P. 70 © 1995 Simshauser Creative.
P. 70 © 1995 David Lomeli/Man?Bot! Design.
P. 71 © DogStar.
P. 72 © 1995 Pace Design Group. All rights reserved.
P. 73 © Rick Sealock.
P. 74 © Swieter Design USA.
P. 75 © Barbara Bruch Design.
P. 76 © 1995 Peterson & Company.
P. 77 © 1995 Sheehan Design.
P. 78 © Paula Brinkman.
P. 79 © 1990, 1995 Gunnar Swanson.
P. 82 © 1995 Modern Dog.
P. 83 © KINETIK Communications Graphics, Inc.
P. 84 © Tarzan Communications Inc.
P. 85 © Segura Inc.
P. 86 © Sackett Design Associates, San Francisco/ Kansas City.
P. 87 © 1995 Modern Dog.
P. 88 © 1994 Jon Dilley Applied Arts.
P. 89 © 1995 Sayles Graphic Design.
P. 90 © Mires Design.
P. 91 © Segura Inc.
P. 92 © 1994 Hansen Design Company.
P. 92 © Tarzan Communications Inc.
P. 93 © 1995 Mitten Design.
P. 94 © 1995 GoodNet, Inc.
P. 95 © Sagmeister Inc.
P. 96 © After Hours Creative.
P. 97 © Aileen Farnan Antonier.
P. 98 © Kilmer, Kilmer and James, Inc.
P. 99 © KINETIK Communications Graphics, Inc.
P. 100 © Two Dimensions Inc.
P. 101 © Toni Schowalter Design.
P. 102 © 1995 Hansen Design Company.
P. 103 © Vaughn/Wedeen Creative.
P. 104 © 1995 Coulter Design and Yankee Title Associates.
P. 105 © Love Packaging Group.
P. 106 © Vaughn/Wedeen Creative.
P. 107 © NextLink and Hornall Anderson Design Works, Inc.
P. 108-9 © Segura Inc.
P. 110 © Matsumoto Incorporated.
P. 111 © Segura Inc.
P. 114 © plus design inc.
P. 115 © Sagmeister Inc.
P. 116 © Delessert and Marshall and Etienne Delessert.
P. 117 © Delessert and Marshall.
P. 118 © Studio Lúmen.
P. 119 © 1995 Sayles Graphic Design.
P. 120 © 1995 KODE Associates, Inc.
P. 121 © 1995 Rick Eiber Design.
P. 122 © Antista Fairclough Design.
P. 123 © 1995 Gee + Chung Design.
P. 124 © Studio Lúmen.
P. 125 © AquaPenn Spring Water Company.
P. 126 © Matsumoto Incorporated.
P. 127 © 1995 Culinary Arts and Entertainment.
P. 128 © 1995 Greteman Group.
P. 129 © Alan Jackson.
P. 130 © Mires Design.
P. 131 © Matsumoto Incorporated.
P. 132 © Matsumoto Incorporated.
P. 133 © Hasegawa Enterprise Ltd., Tokyo, Japan.
P. 134 © 1995 Greteman Group.
P. 135 © Brew Moon Enterprises, Inc.
P. 136 © 1995 Eric Thoelke/Von Tress Architects.
P. 137 © Sagmeister Inc.
P. 138 © 1995 Eagle River Communications.

Directory of Design Firms

After Hours Creative
1201 E. Jefferson, Ste. B100
Phoenix, AZ 85034

Antista Fairclough Design
64B Lenox Pointe NE
Atlanta, GA 30324

Barbara Bruch Design
609A Custer Ave.
Evanston, IL 60202

Belyea Design Alliance
1809 Seventh Ave., Ste. 1007
Seattle, WA 98101

The Bradford Lawton
Design Group
719 Ave. E
San Antonio, TX 78215

Paula Brinkman
417 W. 43 St., #12
New York, NY 10036

Callahan & Co.
9 W. 29th St.
Baltimore, MD 21218

Coulter Design
81 Hayes St., #3
New Britain, CT 06053-2813

Delessert and Marshall
P.O. Box 1689
5 Lakeview Ave.
Lakeville, CT 06039

DogStar
626 54th St. S.
Birmingham, AL 35212

Dyer/Mutchnick Group, Inc.
8360 Melrose Ave., 3rd Floor
Los Angeles, CA 90069

Eric Kass
11523 Cherry Blossom East
Drive
Fishers, IN 46038

Gee + Chung Design
38 Bryant St., Ste. 100
San Francisco, CA 94105

Greteman Group
142 N. Mosley
Wichita, KS 67202

Gunnar Swanson Design Office
916 E. 3rd St., #110
Duluth, MN 55805-2139

Hal Apple Design &
Communication
1112 Ocean Dr., Ste. 203
Manhattan Beach, CA 90266

Hansen Design Company
1809 7th Ave., Ste. 1709
Seattle, WA 98101

Hornall Anderson Design
Works, Inc.
1008 Western Ave., Ste. 600
Seattle, WA 98104

Industrial Strength Design
184 E. 2nd St., Ste. 4E
New York, NY 10009

John Brady Design
Consultants
3 Gateway Center, 17th Floor
Pittsburgh, PA 15222-1012

Jon Dilley Applied Arts
4433 Roanoke, #1N
Kansas City, MO 64111

Kilmer, Kilmer & James Inc.
125 Truman NE, #200
Albuquerque, NM 87106

KINETIK Communication
Graphics, Inc.
1604 17th Street NW, 2nd fl.
Washington, DC 20009

Kode Associates, Inc.
54 W. 22nd St.
New York, NY 10010

Lance Anderson Design
22 Margrave Pl., Studio 5
San Francisco, CA 94133

Love Packaging Group
410 E. 37th St. N., Plant 2,
Graphics Dept.
Wichita, KS 67219

Man?Bot! Design
1124 Cypress Dr.
Vista, CA 92084

Masi Graphica Ltd.
4244 N. Bell
Chicago, IL 60618

Matsumoto Incorporated
220 W. 19th St., 9th Floor
New York, NY 10011

Maverick Art Tribe
112C 17th Ave. NW
Calgary, Alberta
T2M OM6, CANADA

May & Co.
5401 North Central
Expressway, Ste. 325
Dallas, TX 75205

Mike Salisbury Communications
2200 Amapola Ct., Ste. 202
Torrance, CA 90501

Mires Design, Inc.
2345 Kettner Blvd.
San Diego, CA 92101

Mitten Design
604 Mission St., Ste. 820
San Francisco, CA 94105

Modern Dog
7903 Greenwood Ave. N.
Seattle, WA 98103

Nesnadny + Schwartz
10803 Magnolia Dr.
Cleveland, OH 44106

Nicholas Associates
213 W. Institute Pl., Ste. 704
Chicago, IL 60610

Pace Design Group
665 3rd St., Ste. 250
San Francisco, CA 94107

Peterson & Company
2200 N. Lamar, Ste. 310
Dallas, TX 75202

Phoenix Creative
611 N. 10th St.
St. Louis, MO 63101

Pierson Hawkins Inc. Advertising
7555 E. Hampden Ave.,
Ste. 510
Denver, CO 80231

plus design inc.
25 Drydock Ave.
Boston, MA 02210

Reuter Design
657 Bryant St.
San Francisco, CA 94107

Rick Eiber Design (RED)
31014 SE 58th
Preston, WA 98050

The Riordon Design Group Inc.
131 George St.
Oakville, Ontario
L6J 3B9, CANADA

Sackett Design Associates
2103 Scott St.
San Francisco, CA 94115

Sagmeister Inc.
222 W. 14th St.
New York, NY 10011

Sayles Graphic Design
308 8th St.
Des Moines, IA 50309

Segura Inc.
1110 N. Milwaukee Ave.
Chicago, IL 60622

Sheehan Design
2505 2nd Ave., #700
Seattle, WA 98121

Simshauser Creative
60 Tower Hill Dr.
Hanover, MA 02339

Sommese Design
481 Glenn Rd.
State College, PA 16803

Studio Lúmen
Rua Marechal Deodoro, 503
Cj. 1405/1406
Curitiba Paraná Brazil
CEP 80.020-320

Studio MD
1512 Alaskan Way
Seattle, WA 98101

Swieter Design
3227 McKinney, Ste. 201
Dallas, TX 75204

Tarzan Communications Inc.
20 Marie-Anne Ouest
Montreal, Quebec
H2W 1B5, CANADA

TeamDesign, Inc.
1809 7th Ave., Ste. 500
Seattle, WA 98101

Toni Schowalter Design
1133 Broadway, Ste. 1610
New York, NY 10010

Two Dimensions Inc.
88 Advance Rd., Etobicoke,
Ontario, M8Z 2T7, CANADA

Vaughn/Wedeen Creative
407 Rio Grande NW
Albuquerque, NM 87104

Vrontikis Design Office
2021 Pontius Ave.
Los Angeles, CA 90025

Got some fresh ideas of your own that you'd like to share with us?

If you'd like to be put on our mailing list to receive a call for entries for future Fresh Ideas books, please copy the form below (or include the same information in a note to us) and send it to

> Lynn Haller
> Fresh Ideas mailing list
> North Light Books
> 1507 Dana Ave.
> Cincinnati, OH 45207

or call Lynn Haller at (513) 531-2222, or fax her at (513) 531-4744.

Who knows—maybe you'll see your own work in the next Fresh Ideas book!

Please put me on your mailing list to receive calls for entries for future Fresh Ideas books.

My name _____

Studio name _____

Address _____

City _____

State_____Zip Code _____

Phone_____

Fax_____

Index of Clients

Index of Design Firms